Learning the Virtues
That Lead You to God

Also available from
Sophia Institute Press
by Romano Guardini:

The Art of Praying
Eternal Life
The Living God
The Lord's Prayer
Preparing Yourself for Mass
The Rosary of Our Lady

Romano Guardini

Learning the Virtues
That Lead You to God

SOPHIA INSTITUTE PRESS®
Manchester, New Hampshire

Learning the Virtues That Lead You to God was originally published in 1963 by Werkbund-Verlag, Würzburg, Germany, under the title *Tugenden: Meditationen über Gestalten Sittlichen Lebens*. In 1967, Henry Regnery Company published an English translation by Stella Lange titled *The Virtues: On Forms of Moral Life*. This 1998 edition by Sophia Institute Press uses the 1967 Regnery translation, with slight revisions throughout the text.

Cover design by Carolyn McKinney.
Cover art: *Tree of Life*, Currier & Ives, c1892.

Nihil Obstat: Rev. Thomas F. Sullivan, *Censor Librorum*
Imprimatur: Rev. Msgr. Francis W. Byrne, Vicar General,
Archdiocese of Chicago, July 11, 1967

Sophia Institute Press
Box 5284, Manchester, NH 03108
1-800-888-9344
www.SophiaInstitute.com
Sophia Institute Press® is a registered trademark of Sophia Institute.

Library of Congress Cataloging-in-Publication Data
Guardini, Romano, 1885-1968.
  [Tugenden]
  Learning the virtues that lead you to God / Romano Guardini.
    p.   cm.
  Previously published under title: The virtues.
  Includes bibliographical references.
  ISBN: 978-1-62282-930-9 (pbk. : alk. paper)
  1. Virtues. 2. Christian ethics—Catholic authors. I. Guardini, Romano,
1885-1968. Virtues. II. Title.
  BV4630.G813   1998
  241'.4 — dc21   97 40647 CIP

Contents

Preface

In Plato's *Republic*, there is a passage in which Socrates demonstrates how the supreme truth is united in "the Good" with the divine itself. In reply, his young interlocutor, Glaucon, cries out in amazement, "You speak of an inconceivably transcendent beauty!"[1]

In regard to the manner in which the great master of philosophic thought makes the state the protector of the moral order, one may well differ with him. We have learned by bitter experience what happens when government officials take into their hands what belongs to personal freedom. There is one thing, however, that Plato's philosophy has made clear once and for all; that is, after the confusion and chaos introduced into thought by the Sophists, he showed that absolute values exist, that these can be known, and that therefore there is such a thing as truth. He likewise showed that these values are summed up in the majesty of that which we call "the Good," and that this good can be realized in the life of man according to the potentialities of each individual. Plato showed

---

[1] Plato (Greek philosopher; 429-347 B.C.), The Republic, Bk. 6, 509b.

that the good is identical with the divine; but that its realization leads man to true humanity, as virtue comes into being, and this virtue signifies perfection of life, freedom, and beauty. All this is everlastingly valid, even for us today.

These are the matters of which we intend to speak in this work. The ensuing reflections — they are purposely called by this name to distinguish them from scholarly treatises — have grown out of the spoken word, and the reception given these talks has shown that our age, in spite of all its skepticism, longs for an interpretation of everyday life based upon the eternal.

This interpretation shall be carried out in a very unsystematic way. The first chapter deals with the determining points of view. Our interpretation does not pretend to be exhaustive. Rather, it lays hold upon ordinary reality as it came to our attention and seeks therein the starting points of moral self-realization. At all points, it appeals to the personal experience of the reader and strives from there to progress to a unity of ethical consciousness.

Moral teaching has become too negative; these reflections seek to do justice to the living majesty, nobility, and beauty of the good. We tend too much to view the ethical norm as external to rebellious man; here we shall regard the good as that whose realization makes man truly human. The young Glaucon was seized by a reverent transport at the words of his master. This book would attain its purpose if the reader felt that the knowledge of the good is a cause of joy.

In 1930, a collection of "Letters on Self-Culture," which had been composed during the preceding years, was made and published in book form. These letters were addressed to young people and in many ways presupposed the atmosphere of the

Youth Movement. The present reflections are addressed to the more mature and presuppose a knowledge of the bitter years which we have experienced since that time. A historical abyss separates these two attempts at a doctrine of life, and yet they belong together, as in the same man, youth and maturity belong together.

As regards the final chapter, "Justice Before God," the reader would do well if, after taking note of it, he reconsidered the preceding reflections in the light of the points made in it.

Editor's note: The biblical references in the following pages are based on the Douay-Rheims version of the Old and New Testaments. Where applicable, quotations have been cross-referenced with the differing names and enumeration in the Revised Standard Version, using the following symbol: (RSV =).

*Learning the Virtues
That Lead You to God*

The Nature of Virtue

In these reflections, we shall deal with something that concerns us all, each in his own way, namely, virtue. The word probably affects us strangely, perhaps even unfavorably; it is likely to sound old-fashioned and "preachy."

Forty years ago, the philosopher Max Scheler wrote an essay entitled "Toward the Rehabilitation of Virtue."[2] This title is a bit strange, but understandable, if we consider that at that time, ethics, which under the rule of Kant[3] had petrified and become merely a doctrine of duties, was loosening up, and people were beginning once again to think of the good as something living, which concerns the whole man. In that situation, Scheler pointed out the changes that the word and the concept *virtue* had undergone in the course of history until they took on the wretchedly deficient character which still clings to them.

For the Greek, virtue, *areté*, was the nature of the noble-minded and culturally developed man; for the Roman, *virtus*

---

[2] Max Scheler, "On the Reversal of Values," collected works (Bern: 1955), III, 13 ff.

[3] Immanuel Kant (1724-1804), German philosopher.

signified the firmness and solidity which the noble man maintained in public and private life; the Middle Ages understood by *virtue* (*tugent*), the conduct of the chivalrous man. But gradually this virtue became well-behaved and useful, until it received the curious tone which causes aversion in the normal man.

If our language had another word, we would use it. But it has only this one; therefore we want to begin by agreeing that *virtue* denotes something living and beautiful.

Then, what does it mean? It means that the motives, the powers, the actions, and the being of man are gathered at any given time into a characteristic whole by a definitive moral value, an ethical dominant, so to speak.

Let us choose as an example a very modest virtue, such as orderliness. This means that a person knows where a thing belongs and what is the proper time for an action, and also what measure is valid in any instance and what is the relation of the various matters of life to each other. It indicates a sense of rule and recurrence and a feeling for what is necessary so that a condition or an arrangement may endure. When orderliness becomes a virtue, the person who practices it does not wish to realize it only in a single decision — for instance, if he ought to work and instead would like to do something else, he pulls himself together and does what the occasion requires. Orderliness becomes an attitude of his whole life, a disposition which prevails everywhere and determines not only his personal actions but even his surroundings, so that his whole environment acquires a quality of clarity and reliability.

But the virtue of orderliness, in order to be a living thing, must also touch the other virtues. So that a life may be ordered in the proper way, this orderliness must not become a yoke which burdens and constrains; rather it must contribute to growth. Hence it includes a consciousness of what hinders life and what facilitates it. So a personality is rightly ordered if it possesses energy and can overcome itself, but also if it is capable of breaking a rule when, for example, this is necessary to avoid being cramped.

A true virtue signifies an ability to penetrate with a glance the whole existence of man. Within it, as we have said, one ethical value becomes dominant and gathers together the living fullness of the personality.

Now, there are two ways in which the virtue of orderliness is realized. It may be innate; then it comes forth easily and self-evidently from the nature of the person in question. Everyone probably knows such a person, whose desk is always clear and at whose touch things seem to find their place of their own accord. The task of such a person consists in cultivating his native quality and developing it so that it becomes a matter of course which makes existence clear and fair. But he must also guard against a degeneration, for an excess of orderliness can make one hard and narrow. It can produce the pedant, around whom life dries out.

But there are also persons of a different disposition, for whom orderliness is not a quality of nature. They are inclined to follow the impulse of the moment, and in consequence their actions lack consistency. They leave off what they have begun because it is boring; they let objects lie as they fell because they are in a hurry to get away. Indeed, order as such annoys them. They consider a neat room uncomfortable; to look ahead over the day and apportion it seems to them pedantic; to account for receipts and expenses and to balance them seems an irksome constraint. The fact that there is a rule irritates them and stirs the desire to break it, because for them freedom means the possibility of always doing just what their feelings urge them to do. Persons of this type can attain orderliness only through their understanding of the fact that it is an indispensable element of life, the life of the person and of the community. They must discipline themselves, begin again after each failure and do battle for orderliness. In this way, the character of the virtue in them is something conscious and toilsome, eventually reaching a certain degree of naturalness, but always endangered.

Both of these forms of virtue are good, and both are necessary. It is as great a mistake to think that only that virtue is genuine which springs naturally from one's disposition as it is to say that only that is ethical which is acquired with pain and toil. Both are virtue, morally formed humanity, but only realized in different ways.

We might also point out that proper order takes on a different character according to the sphere with which it deals. Lifeless objects in a warehouse are ordered differently than, let us say, living beasts in a stable, or persons in an industry; soldiers in service are ordered differently than children in school.

So a great many things might be said on the subject. In connection with the feeling for human worth and social position, the sense of order results in a proper behavior in social life, together with a sensitivity to situations, a feeling for what is proper, tact, etc.

Virtue is also a matter of our attitude toward the world. How does a person in whom the feeling for order has become effective view the world? He observes that everything in it is "ordered according to measure, number and weight,"[4] as Scripture says. He knows that nothing happens by chance and that everything has a meaning and connection. He rejoices at the sight of this order. He may think, for instance, of the cosmology of the Pythagoreans, who equated the laws of the cosmos with those of musical harmony and said that what guided the course of events was the sound of Apollo's lyre.

He who has this disposition sees also the order in history, sees that profound laws prevail there, that everything has its cause and nothing is without effect. The Greeks expressed this by the concept of *themis*, according to which all human activity is regulated by divine law and justice. Consequently, this virtue signifies a relation to the whole of existence and enables us to discover aspects of it which never become clear to the one who lives in disorder.

Of course, this orderly view may also become rigid so that it sees order merely as natural order and even this as only a mechanical necessity. Then the original form and living productiveness disappear; as does all that may be called spiritual fullness, freedom, and creativity; and existence congeals in dull and soundless inevitability.

But a person sensitive to order can also suffer in consequence. Indeed every genuine virtue entails a predisposition to spiritual joy and also to spiritual suffering. The disorderly person remains indifferent to the confusion of human affairs, insofar as they do not affect him personally, or he may even consider them his native element and enjoy them. But he who

---

[4] Wisd. 11:20.

knows the meaning of order senses the danger, even the sinister quality, of disorder. This may be expressed in the ancient concept of chaos, the destruction of existence. Form has become formlessness in the monster, the dragon, the werewolf, and the midgardserpent. Here we see the nature of the true hero (Gilgamesh,[5] Heracles,[6] Siegfried[7]) who does not go forth to seek adventure or glory, but knows that it is his task to overcome chaos. They conquer that which makes the world monstrous, and unlivable; they create freedom and suitable conditions for life. For him who desires order, every disorder in the interior life of man, in human relations, in his lifework, and in the state is alarming, and can even be a torment.

Virtue may also become morbid. We have already touched on that point. Order may become a shackle by which man suffers harm. I knew a very talented man who said, "When I have once made up my mind to do something, I would not be able to alter my decision even if I wished to do so." In this case, order has become compulsion. Or we may think of the scrupulousness of conscience which torments a man with the feeling that he must do something and do it again and again, endlessly, compelled by an urge that never leaves him. Then there is the teacher who forces everything into rigid rules in order to remain master of his pupils, because he is unable to create an elastic order which serves the purposes of life. And there is also the pathological condition in which a person feels, "Now is the time, now 'it' must be done, or something terrible will

[5] Hero of Sumerian and Babylonian epics.
[6] Hercules, the hero of classical myth who possessed exceptional strength.
[7] Hero of Richard Wagner's opera *The Ring of the Nibelungs*.

happen," but he does not know what it is that must be done. Here we have a compulsion to order which has lost its content.

In every virtue, there is the possibility of constraint. Therefore man must become master, even of his virtue, in order to attain to the freedom of the image of God.

Virtue extends through the whole of existence, as a harmony which gathers it into unity. And it also ascends to God, or rather it descends from Him.

Plato already knew this, when he invented for God the name of *Agathon*, "the Good." It is from the eternal goodness of God that moral enlightenment comes into the soul of the receptive man. It imparts to different characters their respective dispositions for good. This understanding reaches its perfection in the Christian Faith. We may recall the mysterious vision in Revelation where the embodiment of order, the Holy City, comes down from God to man.[8] Due to the limitations of space, we shall mention only a few fundamental points.

First of all, there is a truth, a reality upon which every order of existence depends. It is the fact that God alone is God and that man is His creature and image — that God is really God, not an anonymous principle of the universe, not a mere idea, not the mystery of existence, but He who is Himself the real and living one, Lord and Creator, and man is His creature and is obliged to obey the supreme Lord.

This is the basic order of all earthly conditions and earthly activity. Against it, the first man rebelled when he let himself be persuaded that he might "be as God,"[9] and this rebellion

---

[8] Rev. 21:10 ff.
[9] Cf. Gen. 3:5.

continues to the present day, on the part of great and small, genius and gabbler. But if this order is disturbed, then no matter how much power is gained, how much welfare secured, or how much culture developed, all things remain in chaos.

Another way in which the virtue of order is established by God is the irrevocable law that all wrong demands expiation. Man likes to attribute his own forgetfulness to history and thinks that, when he has done wrong, things continue undisturbed: the intended effects remain, and the wrong is past, is annihilated. A concept of the state has grown up, according to which the state is permitted any wrong for the purposes of power, prosperity, and progress. If these ends are attained, the wrong is blotted out.

As a matter of fact, the wrong is still there, in the matter and the continuity of history, in the lives of those who have committed it and in those who have suffered it, in the influence it has had upon others, and in the impression upon the opinions, the language, and the attitudes which characterize the age. And it shall be expiated some day; it must be expiated — inescapably. God vouches for that.

The third point is the revelation of the judgment. History is not a natural process which is self-justified; rather, it must render an account, but not to public opinion or to science and scholarship. It is likewise incorrect to say that the course of history is itself the judgment, for much remains hidden, much forgotten, and the responsibility for many things is placed where it does not belong. No, judgment is reserved for God. Everything will come before His truth and will be revealed. Everything will come under His justice and receive His final verdict.

We see that what we have called the "virtue of order," which at first appeared so commonplace, reaches ever deeper, becomes more and more inclusive and finally ascends to God Himself — and descends from Him to men. This concatenation is what the word *virtue* means.

In the following, we shall work out a series of such structures of man's relation to the good. We shall do this without any system, but rather we shall use image upon image as these present themselves in the manifold varieties of human experience. This will help us to understand man better, to see more clearly how he lives, how life becomes his task, and how he performs it meaningfully or gambles it away.

This will also help us in the practical conduct of our own life. For there is a relation of choice between our various predispositions to the different virtues. These are not a general pattern to be imposed on men, but are themselves living humanity, insofar as it hears the appeal of the good and fulfills itself therein. And the good is a living treasure, radiating from God, at its source infinitely rich and yet simple, but breaking up and unfolding at its contact with human existence.

Every virtue is a diffraction of this infinitely rich simplicity upon a potentiality of man. But that means that different individuals according to their potentiality are more or less related or alien to the different virtues. So a socially inclined person who readily establishes relations with others will find the virtue of understanding quite easy and natural, whereas it is naturally strange to the active resolute person fixed upon his goal. A person of creative temperament has an originality which enables him to grasp a given situation vividly, while the person who is of more logical temper holds to fixed rules.

Learning the Virtues

To see all this is important for our understanding of the moral life of different individuals. It is also important for our own daily life, because in our moral development, it is well to begin with that which is familiar to us and then to advance to the conquest of that which is more alien.

Truthfulness

A virtue which has suffered great damage in our day is truthfulness, which, taken in its widest interpretation, includes also the love of truth, and the will that truth should be recognized and accepted.

First, truthfulness means that the speaker should say what is so, as he sees and understands it, and that he should express what is in his mind. Under certain circumstances, this may be difficult, and may even cause annoyance, harm, and danger. But our conscience reminds us that truth is an obligation, that it is something absolute and sublime. It is not something of which we may say, "You may tell it if it is convenient for you or serves some purpose," but, "When you speak, you must tell the truth, not abbreviate it or change it. You must tell it absolutely, simply — unless the situation urges you to be silent or you can evade a question in a decent and proper way."

But apart from this, our whole existence depends upon truth. We shall say more about this later. The relations of people to each other, social institutions, and government — all that we call civilization and man's work in its countless forms — depend on a respect for truth.

Truthfulness means, then, that man has the instinctive feeling that the truth must be told, absolutely. Of course — we must emphasize this point again — this obligation is based upon the assumption that the questioner has the right to be informed. If he does not, then it becomes the task of experience and prudence to find the proper way of avoiding an answer.

We must also note that in regard to truthfulness in daily life, it makes a difference if one possesses interior certainty in regard to the various situations, and also if one is a master of the language and quick to define and distinguish. This is a matter of ethical culture with which education should deal. Many a lie arises from shyness and embarrassment, and also from insufficient mastery of the language.

Special problems arise from circumstances such as we have known in the past and still meet today, when a totalitarian tyranny places all under compulsion and permits no personal convictions. Then man is perpetually on the defensive. Those who exercise violence have no right to demand the truth, and they know that they cannot expect it. Violence causes speech to lose its meaning. It becomes a means of self-protection for the one who is violated, unless the situation is such that it demands a testimony by which the speaker risks property and life. To determine this is the affair of conscience, and he who lives in secure freedom may well consider whether he has a right to pass judgment in such a case.

At any rate, truthfulness means that one tells the truth, not only once but again and again, so that it becomes a habit. It brings to the whole man, his being and his action, something clear and firm.

And one should not only *speak* the truth but should *do* it, for one can lie also through actions, attitudes, and gestures, if these seem to express something which is not so.

But truthfulness is something more. We have already spoken of the fact that virtue is never isolated. Surely we have already observed that nature does not know the absolutely "pure" tone, that there are always overtones and undertones forming a chord. A pure color also does not occur, but only a mixture of colors. Similarly, "bare" truthfulness cannot exist. It would be hard and unjust. What exists is living truthfulness, which other elements of the good penetrate and affect.

There are persons who are truthful by nature. They are too orderly to be able to lie, too much in harmony with themselves — sometimes we may even say too proud to lie. This is a splendid thing in itself. But such a person is often in danger of saying things at the wrong time, of offending or hurting others. A truth that is spoken at the wrong moment or in a wrong way may so confuse a person that he has difficulty in getting his bearings again. That would not be a living truthfulness but a one-sided one, damaging and destructive. Of course, there are moments when one must not look to the right or left, but state the plain truth. But, as a rule, it holds good that we are in the context of existence, and here consideration for the other person is as important as truth-telling. Therefore truth-telling, in order to attain its full human value, must be accompanied by tact and kindness.

Truth is not spoken into a vacuum but to another person; therefore the speaker must try to understand what its effect will be. St. Paul makes a statement whose full meaning is untranslatable: he says that those whom he is addressing, the

Christians of Ephesus, should *aletheuein en agape*. Here the noun *aletheia* is turned into a verb: "to speak, to do, to be truth," but "in love."[10] In order that truth may come to life, love must accompany it.

On the other hand, there are persons in whom this feeling for others is very strongly developed. They perceive immediately how they feel; understand their nature and situation; are aware of their needs, apprehensions, and troubles; and consequently are in danger of giving in to the influence of these conditions. Then they not only show consideration, but adapt themselves; they weaken the truth or overemphasize it, indicate a parity of opinion or meaning where it really does not exist. Indeed, the influence can predispose their own way of thinking, so that not only external independence of speech and action is lost, but even the interior independence of judgment.

Here, too, the living quality of truth is endangered, for it includes the liberty of spirit to see what is true, the determination of responsibility which upholds its judgment even in the face of sympathy and helpfulness, and the strength of personality which understands that its own dignity stands or falls with its loyalty to truth.

So we have two elements which must accompany the desire for truth if the complete virtue is to develop: consideration for the person addressed and courage when truth-telling becomes difficult.

Other things are also necessary. For instance, one needs experience of life and an understanding of its ways. He who

[10]Eph. 4:15.

sees life too simply thinks that he is telling the truth when he may actually be doing violence to it. He may say of another, "He is a coward!" Actually, the other man does not have the forthrightness of one who is sure of himself; he is timid and uncertain and does not dare to act. The judgment seems correct, but the one who pronounces it lacks knowledge of life, or he would have understood the signs of inhibition in the other person.

Again, one may judge that another is bold, whereas he is really shy and is trying to overcome his interior inhibitions.

We might add many other examples. They would lead us to see that living truth claims and requires the whole man. A friend of mine once remarked in conversation, "Truthfulness is the most subtle of all virtues. But there are persons who handle it like a club."

All relations of men with each other, the whole life of the community, depend on faithfulness to truth.

Man is a mysterious being. If someone stands before me, I see his exterior appearance, hear his voice, grasp his hand; but what is going on within him is hidden from me. The more real and vital it is, the more deeply it is buried. So there arises the disturbing fact that the association of persons with each other — and that means the greater part of life — is a relation which moves from one mystery to another. What forms the bridge? The facial expression and gestures, the bearing and actions, but, above all, the word. Through the word, man communicates with man. The more reliable the word, the more secure and fruitful the communication is.

Moreover, human relationships are of varying depth and significance. The gradation passes from mere getting along with one another and man's simple needs, to the life of the soul, to the workings of the mind, the question of responsibility, and the relation of person to person. The way leads ever deeper, into the special, individual, profoundly personal, into the range of freedom where our calculations fail. So the truth of the word becomes ever more important. This is applicable to every kind of relationship — above all to those upon which life in the proper sense depends: friendship, collaboration, love, marriage, and the family. Associations that are to endure, to grow, and to become fruitful must become ever more pure in the truthfulness of each toward the other; if not, they will disintegrate. Every falsehood destroys the community.

But the mystery goes deeper. It does not consist merely in the fact that every communication passes from the hidden depths of one person to those of another, but everyone also communicates with himself. Here man, so to speak, separates into two beings and confronts himself. I consider myself, test and judge myself, and decide about myself. Then this duality again unites into the single self and thereafter bears within itself the results of this encounter. This is constantly happening in the process of the interior life. It is the way in which it is accomplished.

But what if I am not truthful in dealing with myself? What if I deceive myself, pretend? And do we not do this constantly? Is not the man who is always "in the right" most perilously "in the wrong"? Does not the man in whose opinion others are always at fault constantly disregard his own fault? Is not the one who always gets his way living in a tragic delusion, unaware how foolish, conceited, narrow, and brutal he is and what harm he is doing? If I wish to associate properly with myself and so with others, I must not disregard my own reality, must not deceive myself, but must be true in dealing with myself. But how difficult that is, and how deplorable our state if we honestly examine ourselves!

Truth gives man firmness and stability. He has need of these, for life is not only a friend, but also an enemy. Everywhere interests oppose each other. Constantly we meet touchiness, envy, jealousy, and hatred. The very differences of disposition and point of view cause complications. Even the simple fact that there is "the other," for whom I am in turn "the other" is a root of conflict.

How shall I manage? By defending myself, of course. Life is in many respects a battle, and in this battle, falsehood and deceit might sometimes seem useful. But what on the whole gives us firmness and strength are truth, honesty, and reliability. These qualities bring about enduring results: respect and confidence.

This is also true in regard to that great power which penetrates the whole of man's life and which is called "the state." It is no accident that whenever the state, whose basic principles should be liberty and justice, becomes a tyranny, lying and falsehood grow proportionately. Even more, truth is deprived of its value; it ceases to be the norm and is replaced by success. Why? Because it is through truth that the spirit of man is constantly confirmed in its natural rights, and the person is reassured of his dignity and freedom. When a person says, "It is so," and this statement has weight in public because truth is honored, then he is protected against the force inherent in every government. But if the government succeeds in depriving truth of its value, then the individual is helpless.

The most hideous manifestation of tyranny occurs when a man's conscience and consciousness of truth are broken, so that he is no longer able to say, "This is so . . . this is not so." Those who bring this about — in political and judicial affairs, or elsewhere — should realize clearly what they are doing: they are depriving man of his humanity. This realization would crush and destroy them.

Truth is also the means by which man becomes stable and attains character. This is determined by the fact that a man's nature has taken on that firmness which is expressed by these statements: "What is, is. What is right, must be done. What has been entrusted to me, I uphold." In the measure in which this comes about, man gains stability and self-reliance.

But is this not self-evident? Does not everyone possess stability by the mere fact that he is himself — as every animal is itself; the swallow, a swallow and the fox, a fox?

Here we must not be careless in our thinking, for much depends upon exactness in these matters. Why does an animal make so strong an impression of stability, of being at one with itself? This is so because it is "nature," a living being without a personal soul. The "spiritual" element within it — order, meaningful being, and behavior — is the spirit of the Creator, not its own. But man possesses a spiritual soul, a free and rational personality. Through this he is worlds above the animal, but for this very reason, he lacks the animal's natural stability and unity. He is endangered by his own spirit, which constantly tries to overstep its own nature and to become self-determined, and thereby also to question and deceive itself. If we add to this all that Faith tells us about the disorder caused by Original Sin and all that followed, then we see that man is a being endangered by his very origin and that he must constantly resist the evil possibilities within himself. From this point of view, man "is" not simply himself, his true self, but he is on the way toward it and seeking it. And when he acts rightly, he "becomes" himself.

How important it is, then, to ask what is the way in which a true selfhood comes into being, in the profoundest depths of existence, beyond all tensions and disturbances. The answer — above all answers that could be given — is this: it comes from the will to truth. In every true thought and word and deed, the interior center, the true self, is confirmed, imperceptibly but really. How dangerous it is when man is deceived about his own nature, in speech, in literature, and in pictures. Often we say to ourselves in terror: "That which science, literature, politics, newspapers, and films call man is not really man at all. It is an illusion or an assertion for some ulterior motive, or a weapon, or simply thoughtlessness."

Our considerations have advanced far. We said in our first reflection that every virtue involves the whole man. This has been confirmed again. Indeed the virtue extends far beyond man, to God.

Let us just think deeply about this: if I say, "Two and two are four," I know that it is wholly four and only four and always four. I know that this is correct and there will never be a moment when it is not correct, unless certain but definite conditions of higher mathematics are involved. What brings about this certainty that cannot be anything but what it is? What is the reason, beyond these simple relations of sense objects, why every true knowledge at the moment of its flashing upon us brings with it the certainty that it is so? Of course

I can err if I have not observed carefully enough or thought clearly enough. That can happen, and it happens every day. But when I really know, then I say, "It is so."

What brings about this strange certainty of the mind depending on nothing tangible? It can only be something that comes from God. Something that does not come from man himself here enters into human action and experience. It is a power, not of compulsive force, but of the reason appealing to us and bearing witness of itself; a power of the mind which brings about that firmness in man which we call "conviction." Plato built his whole philosophy upon this basic experience. He called this power a "light"; the highest, indeed, the real light, that comes from the true sun. This sun is God, whom, as we mentioned before, Plato calls the *Agathon*, "the Good." St. Augustine, relying upon St. John, introduced this idea into Christian thought, where it became eternally fruitful.

In the last analysis, what is truth really? It is the way in which God is God and knows Himself, is knowing, and in His knowledge bears Himself. Truth is the indestructible and untouchable solidity with which God, by knowing, is based upon Himself. From Him truth moves into the world and gives it solidity. Truth penetrates all being and gives it its nature; its light shines into the human mind and gives it that brightness which we call "knowledge."

This is a valid conclusion: He who holds to the truth holds to God. He who lies rebels against God and betrays the rational basis of existence.

In this world, the truth is weak. A trifle suffices to hide it. The stupidest persons can attack it. But someday the time will come when things will change. God will bring it about that truth will be as powerful as it is true; and this will be the judgment.

Judgment means that the possibility of lying ceases because omnipotent truth penetrates every mind, illumines every word, and rules in every place. Then falsehood will be revealed as what it is. However expedient, clever, or elegant it may have been, it will be exposed as an illusion, as a nonentity.

We should let these thoughts occupy our minds, our understanding, and our hearts. Then we shall perhaps sense what truth is, its steadfastness, its calm radiance, and its nobility. Then we will enter into union with it, through all that is most intimate and loyal within us. We will accept responsibility for the truth and expend our efforts in its behalf.

All this will suffer opposition and trials, because we are human. But our lives must testify to the fact that truth is the basis of everything: of the relation of man to man, of man to himself, of the individual to the community, and above all, of man to God — no, of God to us.

Acceptance

If someone should ask, "I would like to make progress in moral life; where shall I begin?" then we would probably answer, "Wherever you will. You can begin with a fault of which you have become conscious in your profession or occupation. Or else you can begin with the needs of the community, with family or friends — wherever you have ascertained a failing. Or else you may be aware that some passion has power over you, and you may strive to overcome it. Basically, all that matters is that you should be honest and sincere and make a determined effort."

Then one thing will lead to another. For the life of man is a whole. If he grasps it anywhere with determination, then his conscience awakens and strengthens his moral power in other respects as well, just as a fault anywhere in his life makes its influence felt everywhere.

But if the questioner urges us further, "What is the presupposition for all moral effort if it is to be effective, to change what is amiss, to strengthen what is feeble, and to balance what is uneven?" then, I believe, we would have to answer, "It is the acceptance of what is, the acceptance of reality, your own and that of the people around you and of the time in which you live."

Perhaps this sounds somewhat theoretical, yet it is not only correct but deserves the special attention of everyone who is making an honest effort; for it is by no means self-evident that we accept what is, accept it interiorly, with a ready heart. Someone might object again and say, "But this is affectation. What is, is, whether we 'accept' it or not, quite apart from the fact that such a disposition is very convenient and must lead to passivity." So we must make it clear at once that we are not dealing with a weak submissiveness, but with seeing the truth and taking one's stand upon it, resolved, of course, to work for it and, if necessary, to fight for it.

Here true humanity begins. An animal is essentially in harmony with itself. More accurately, for the animal the question does not exist. It is naturally adapted to its environment just as it is and is absorbed in it. That is why it gives us the impression of "naturalness." It is exactly as it must be according to its nature and the surrounding conditions.

Man's situation is different. He is not absorbed in his own being and environment. He can depart from himself and think about himself. He can judge himself and can raise his desires above what he is to that which he would like to be or should be. Indeed, he can lift himself in fancy to the impossible. So there arises a tension between his actual being and his desires, which may become a principle of growth insofar as he keeps before him in his striving an image of himself, which he seeks to overtake with that which he really is. But the tension may also cause a harmful split, a flight from one's own reality, a fantasy existence which disregards the given possibilities and also the threatening dangers. This is what we meant when we said that all effective moral striving must begin with a man's sincere acceptance of existence as it is.

Let us try to understand what this acceptance means by seeking to understand more clearly what it is that we accept.

There is first of all myself. For I am not man in general, but this particular person. I have a certain character and no other, a certain temperament among all of the various ones that exist, certain strong and weak points, definite possibilities and limitations. All this I should accept and build upon as the fundamental basis of my life.

This is, we repeat, by no means self-evident. For there is — and this throws a glaring light on the finiteness of our existence — a disgust with our own being, a protest against ourself. We must remember again that man is not, like an animal, enclosed in himself, but can rise above himself. He can think about how he would like to be. And many a person lives more in a dream world than in the consciousness of his reality. We know, too, the curious activities by which a person tries to slip out of what he is, dressing up, masking, playing. Does not all this indicate the vain but ever renewed attempt to be someone other than we really are? So there appears the command, strict and not easy to fulfill, really to wish to be who we are — convinced that behind this, there is no dull necessity of nature, nor a malicious chance, but the allotment by eternal wisdom.

This means that I must accept not only the strong points that I have, but also the weaknesses; not only the possibilities, but also the limitations. For we strange human beings are so constituted that what supports us also burdens us; what brings security also endangers us. Every mode of being has a positive side and also a negative, and we cannot select.

We have attained great wisdom if we have learned that we cannot pick and select among the foundations of existence, but must accept the whole. This does not mean that we should approve of everything and leave everything unchanged. Certainly not. I can and should work on myself and my life and mold and improve it. First, however, I must admit the existing facts; otherwise everything becomes false.

The person endowed with a keen reason, a practical view, and a firm hand often lacks the creativity of imagination, the beauty of the dream which belongs to the artistic temperament. In return, the latter is burdened with the dark moments of emptiness and discouragement, and the difficulty of adjusting to the real world and its calculations. The person of strong feelings who tastes the joys of existence must also endure its pains and sorrows. No one can expect to keep the one and reject the other, but if he wishes to live true to reality, he must accept his own nature. The person who is cool-headed and can easily shake off unpleasant things does not know the heights and depths of existence.

Again, this does not mean that we should call good what is not so. The bad is bad, evil is evil, and what is ugly should be called ugly. But all efforts to develop the one and overcome the other depend on the assumption that we have first recognized and admitted what is. Consider how many people build up fantasies about themselves and seek to circumvent by lies what really is. They are indignant if we call their attention to a fault and surprised if something goes wrong. The beginning of all effort is the recognition of what is, even if that happens to be one's faults. Only when I honestly take upon myself the burden of my faults do I really become serious, and only then can the work of overcoming them begin.

We must also accept the situation and circumstances of our life as they have been allotted to us. Of course, we can change and improve many things and shape them more according to our wishes, especially if these wishes are definite and the hand that seeks to carry them out is firm. But, basically, the tendencies that have grown out of our earliest years remain and determine what follows. Psychologists say that the fundamental characteristics of a child are fixed by the end of his third or fourth year. These accompany him through his later life, as also do those influences which the persons around him, the social group, the city, and the country have exercised.

Another step is the acceptance of our destiny. Destiny is not accident. It possesses a logical consistency which is determined externally by the connection of events but also internally by the nature and character of the person involved.

The life of the average man will not know the triumphs or the catastrophes experienced by the genius. The man whose talents lie in economics and organization will not be seized by the perplexity and despair that often overwhelm the man of artistic nature, and the latter will not experience the victories and defeats of the man who has the ability to acquire and use power. So the nature of a person forms, as it were, a sieve which permits certain experiences to pass through and retains others.

Even those things which may happen to one — perhaps the lightning which strikes a house during a thunderstorm — will be something different if the owner of the house is madly carried away by his misfortune or has self-control and is able to stand firm. So we may say in a certain sense that the individual possesses in his disposition a preliminary sketch of his destiny. This is not a fixed necessity — this is contradicted by the fact of freedom which again and again, in small things and in great, has its part in building a life — but a direction, a basic character, often a probability of definite events. Again, the important thing is that one accept one's destiny and then work more resolutely in guiding and shaping it.

The life of modern man is governed by an idea which is the counterpart of the fear that grips his nerves; that is, the idea of obtaining security against increasing dangers. Of course, we can do many things in this respect. To mention only one thing, we can calculate how great the life expectancy is in a certain occupation, and how great the percentage of accidents is in another; but, we cannot insure ourselves against life itself. Rather, we must accept it with all that it brings, both great and small, of possibilities of fortune and misfortune.

To accept one's destiny really means to accept oneself and to be true to oneself. This idea took the form of the *amor fati* in pagan skepticism, the "love" of one's own fate, born of defiance. Its Christian form is the assent given to the way that is outlined for us by our own nature, because of our confidence that everything rests upon Divine Providence.

The logical consistency of the thought leads us further, to the point where we do not merely resist pain and misfortune, or, if they cannot be avoided, endure them courageously, but where we accept their bitterness. In order to be able to do that, we must have been taught in the school of Christ, for our nature inclines otherwise. It protests against pain, and, to begin with, we cannot object to that, especially since there is a yielding to pain that grows out of weakness; there is even a morbid desire for it. But mere rejection destroys the meaning of pain for our life. If it is rightly understood and borne, it deepens life, cleanses it, and brings man into harmony with himself, because he comes into harmony with the divine will, which is behind all events.

And finally there is this: Acceptance of self means that I consent simply to be.

This statement sounds odd, as long as all is going well. Then we live on in our own being and action and think no further. But when other times come — times of misfortune, of failure, or of disgust — there is a cleavage between me and myself. I did not confront the possibility of my own existence and decide that I wished to be, but I was cast into being. I came forth from the lives of my parents, of my ancestors, out of the conditions of the age. The event of my birth said to me, "Now you *are*. So live your life." At certain moments, we are intimately aware of what a grace it is to *be*, to be permitted to breathe, to feel, and to work.

But it may happen otherwise, so that our own existence appears to us not in the nature of a gift but of a burden. When our strength fails, the world turns gray, and duties weigh upon us; in times of protracted illness or sorrow, in moments of discouragement or of melancholy, we may protest, "I was not asked. I did not want to be. Why must I?" Then we feel that the requirement that we exist is unreasonable, and that it is an act of the deepest profundity of being to accept our existence. For it can be declined, in a dull and weary fashion, when a person continues to live, merely shrugging his shoulders in resignation, but also in a desperate action, for the number of those who cast away their lives is frighteningly large and seems to be growing. They are those for whom the gift of existence becomes a burden and who are unwilling to carry it, or perhaps are unable, because neither faith nor love teaches them to understand the difficult riddle.

In all this we make no progress with merely human motives. We really should have said this at the beginning of our reflections. For when we considered that we cannot construct our own existence, but only receive it, the next question should have been, "From whom?" And the answer would have been, "From our parents, from the historical situation, and from our ancestors. But ultimately and through all the intermediaries, from God." So we cannot attain to a true acceptance if we do not clearly understand from where we receive our existence: from the blind course of nature, the senselessness of chance, the malice of a demon — or from the pure wisdom and love of God. And we must again and again remind ourselves that the basic revelation of Christ was how God is disposed toward us.

True acceptance is possible only if we have proof upon which we can rely. This we have in the living God. The more closely our life is touched by the thing we must accept, and the more clearly the acceptance involves a conquest of ourself — an interior abandonment of self, as the spiritual masters of the Middle Ages expressed it, a surrender of oneself to that which is — the more we need to understand the nature of the omnipotent intention which is directed toward each one of us.

There is a question which is really foolish, but must be asked, since it helps us in our relations with the transcendent

God: Does He really know what He demands of us, He who has no destiny because there is no power that could impose it upon Him? Must not His dispensations, if we may say so, always come "from above," in Olympic fashion, from the calm aloofness of the unapproachable?

Here revelation tells us of a mystery which is as comforting as it is incomprehensible. In Christ, God laid aside this unapproachability. Through the Incarnation, He stepped into the space which forms a single chain of destiny for him who lives in it. God stepped into history. When the eternal Son became man, He did so in reality, without protection or exception, vulnerable by word and act; woven, like us, into the stifling web of effects that proceed from the confused hearts of men.

Yet there is a difference; for the greater his soul and the deeper his feelings and the more intense his life, the more one is affected by these things. To have a destiny means to suffer; the more capable of suffering one is, the greater is the element of destiny in his life. What vistas of thought does this open to us! What a climax does the concept attain! The Son of God steps into history to atone for our sin and to lead us to new possibilities. He does this prepared for all that would happen to Him, without reservation, without evasion, without resorting to resistance or craft. Men, who have really no power over Him to whom is given "all power in Heaven and on earth,"[11] inflict a bitter destiny upon Him. But this is the form of His Father's will for Him. This will is His own will; to accomplish it is the "food" of His life.[12]

[11]Matt. 28:18.
[12]John 4:34.

So the weight of destiny is transformed into freedom. The highest freedom and the heaviest duty become one. We may recall His mysterious word on the way to Emmaus: "Ought not Christ to have suffered and so to enter into His glory?"[13]

But God is not "the absolute Being" of mere philosophy, but He who is such that His most intimate nature, His love, is expressed in this way. And His sovereignty is that supreme freedom which is able and willing to accomplish it.

Only from this point of view can existence be comprehended and mastered. Not through some philosophy of personality and its relation to the world, but through faith in what God has done and in union with Him. The image for this is the Cross, as He said, "If anyone will come after me, let him deny himself and take up his cross and follow me."[14] Each must take up "his own," which is "sent" him. Then the Master accomplishes in him the mystery of holy freedom.

[13]Luke 24:26.
[14]Matt. 16:24.

Patience

Our first reflection endeavored to remove from the concept of virtue the narrow, moralistic tone that it has acquired in the course of time, and to view it as something living, great, and beautiful. So it might seem strange if the title of the following reflection claims that this description also identifies patience. Is not patience something dull and insignificant, a miserable means by which a narrow life seeks to justify its own poverty?

Therefore we shall begin our consideration on the heights with the Lord of all virtue. For the great example of patience is God, because He is the Omnipotent and Loving One.

Have we ever tried to understand how mysterious it is that God created the world at all? The unbeliever knows nothing of this mystery, for he sees the world as "nature"; that is, as something which simply exists. But even the believer is usually not conscious of it, because he thinks of the creating power of God in a natural way, as the first cause in the series of causes which operate in nature. He has faith, but this faith has not yet determined his way of thinking and feeling. This is still similar to the ordinary way of the age. But as soon as faith penetrates the core of the personality, the nature of the finite becomes mysterious and the question arises, "Why did God create it?"

If we were able to answer that question — really to answer it — then we would know much. But on earth this is impossible, for it would presuppose that we could think from God's point of view, and such knowledge will be given to us only in eternity. Here on earth the question remains unanswered: why He — who is all things, can do all things, and is Lord of all riches — created the world. The world which is indeed great, immeasurable for our mind, but always and absolutely finite. God does not need the world. Of what use is it to Him? What does He do with it? Perhaps these considerations give us some inkling of the roots of divine patience.

For God not only created the world, but He upholds and sustains it. He does not become weary of it. There is a myth which may open our eyes — for myths can do that. There is much truth in them, of course in ambiguous form, so that he who hears them is always in danger either of underrating it or of being misled by it.

An Indian myth tells of Shiva, who fashions all things: in an exuberance of delight, he creates the world, but then grows weary of it, treads it into fragments, and produces another. This suffers the same fate, and creating and destroying continue indefinitely. How impressive is the image of this divinity of impatience. It shows us how different is the relation of the true God to the world.

He creates it — the reason is an unfathomable mystery. In spite of its profusion of powers and forms, it is finite, measured and limited throughout. So it does not "suffice" for God Himself, and can never satisfy His eternal demands. Yet He does not become weary of it. This is the first manifestation of patience; that is, that God does not cast away the world, but keeps it in existence, respects it, and that He, if we may use the expression, is faithful to it, forever.

In this world, there is a being possessing consciousness, inwardness, heart, and mind. This being is man. To him God has entrusted His world, so that it may not merely exist but be experienced. Man should continue God's work with understanding, feeling and love. He should administer the first world and shape it in truth and justice. In this way, the second world shall come into being, the real world that God intends.

But how does man treat the work of God? Anyone who has gained some experience and has looked carefully into history and who does not let himself be blinded by the superstition of progress must be terrified to notice how much disorder there is in the world — how much error and folly, greed, violence, and falsehood, how much crime. All this exists in spite of science, technology, and welfare — or rather, together with it, mixed with it, inextricably confused. It exists even in religion, in men's ideas of the divine, their relations with it, and their defense of it. Modern man is inclined simply to accept everything that happens. He arranges one thing next to the other, derives one from the other, declares everything to be necessary, and calls the whole "history." But he who has learned to distinguish, to call the true, true and the false, false, the right, right and the wrong, wrong, cannot do this and must be frightened to see how man deals with the world.

And yet God does not cast away the badly spoiled creation and form a new one. What a terrible threat we glimpse in the account of the flood. If we look into it more deeply, we discern

Learning the Virtues

the hint of a possibility of universal destruction in the words: "The Lord God repented that He had created man upon the earth."[15] But in God — if we may say this — the *yes* is stronger than the *no*, and He carries the world on, "endures" it through time and eternity.

This attitude of God toward the world is the first patience, absolute patience, possible only because He is the Omnipotent One, because He, who knows no weakness, is the true Lord whom no one threatens, the Eternal One, for whom there is neither fear nor haste. We may recall Jesus' parable of the sower and the seed. The master of the field had sown good wheat, but in the midst of it, the weeds sprang up. His servants came and asked, "Shall we tear the weeds out?" But he answered, "No, otherwise you will tear out the wheat with the weeds. Let both grow. Later the harvest will come, and they will be separated from each other."[16]

This is the patience of the one who could use force but spares, because He is truly Lord, noble and gracious. But man is the image of God; he should imitate Him in this respect also. The world is placed in his hand — the world of things, of persons, and of his own life. He should make of it what God expects, even now, after the weeds have spread their rank growth through everything. Patience is the prerequisite for the growth of the wheat.

Can an animal be impatient? Obviously not; it can be neither impatient nor patient. It is fitted into the interrelation of nature's laws; it lives as it must live and dies when its time

[15]Gen. 6:6.
[16]Matt. 13:24-30.

has come. Impatience becomes possible only for a being which is capable of rising above the immediately existing and of desiring what has not yet come to be. It is possible only for man. Only he is faced with the decision whether he is able to allow time for growth and development.

And this must be done again and again, for in this existence in time and finiteness, we constantly find the tension between what man is and what he would like to be; between that which has been realized and that which remains to be accomplished. And it is patience which endures the tension.

It is patience, above all, with that which is given and apportioned to us, our destiny. The environment in which we live is allotted to us; we are born into it. The events of history continue without our being able to change them essentially, and everyone feels their effects. Personally we experience, day by day, what happens to come along. We can resist or change many things according to our wishes; but basically we must accept what comes and is given to us. To understand this and to act accordingly is patience. Anyone who is unwilling to do this is in constant conflict with his own existence.

Let us recall that character who rebels against all laws, Goethe's Faust.[17] After he has renounced hope and faith, he cries out, "And cursed above all be patience!" He is the ever-immature one who never sees reality or accepts it as it is. He always flies above it in his fancy. He is always in a state of protest against his destiny, whereas the maturity of man begins

[17]Johann Wolfgang von Goethe (1749-1832), German poet and dramatist. Faust, a figure in several dramatic works, including Goethe's, is a magician and astrologer who sells his soul to the Devil in exchange for worldly experience and power.

with his acceptance of what is, of reality. Only this gives him the power to change and to reshape it.

We must also have patience with the people who are associated with us, whether it be our parents, husband or wife or child, a friend or a fellow worker, or whoever it may be. Mature, responsible life begins with our accepting people as they are.

It can be very difficult to be bound to a person whom one gradually comes to know intimately: how he speaks, how he thinks, and what his attitude toward everything is. One would like to put him away and take another. Faithfulness here is pre-eminently patience with what he is, how he is and acts, and what he does. If this patience is not exercised, everything goes to pieces and the possibilities that lay in the relationship are lost.

But we must also have patience with ourselves. We know to some extent, in the form of a more or less definite wish, how we should like to be. We would like to be rid of one charac-teristic, or to possess another, and we are annoyed at being just what we are. It is difficult to be obliged to remain the person we are, humiliating always to find in ourselves the same faults, weaknesses, and deficiencies.

Disgust with oneself: the greatest spirits have most often felt this. Here patience must again take over and help us to accept ourselves and to persevere. We are not to approve of that in ourselves which is not good; not to be self-satisfied — that would be the way of the Philistine. Dissatisfaction with our own imperfection and insufficiency must remain; other-wise, we would lose that power of self-criticism which is the prerequisite for all moral development. But it should not cause us to escape into illusions about ourselves. Every sound criticism must begin with what is given and work on from that point, knowing that it will be slow work, extremely slow. And this very slowness guarantees that the change is taking place not in our fancy, but in reality.

Wherein does the moral life consist?

Perhaps we have realized that we lack self-control. We must keep a firmer hold on ourselves, become more quiet in speaking, more prudent in action. We recognize and admit this, but it is at first only in our mind, as a thought or a plan. It must be worked out in real life, and that is difficult.

We may dream ourselves into a virtue, and how much wishful thinking consists of imaginary virtues! But the dreams vanish and everything is as it was — no, it is worse: fantasy consumes moral energy, apart from the lack of truthfulness that is inherent in it. How often, under the impression of a lofty moment or a new resolution, we think, "Now I've made the grade!" But on the next occasion, we notice that our own reality, which seemed to have taken on the form of that which we know to be right, slips back into the old way, and everything is as it was.

A real moral growth would take place if our acts of restraint and self-moderation became more conscious, if our awareness of what our violence might bring about increased, and if we did not let ourselves be carried away so easily by the impulse of our feelings, but remained more free, and attained a mastery over our emotions and our inner selves. This would not be fantasy, but real processes of the interior life, changes in the relation of various acts to each other, the molding of their character. But that sort of thing takes place slowly, very slowly.

Therefore patience, which always begins again, is a pre-requisite if something is really to be done. In *The Imitation of Christ* we find the phrase *"Semper incipe!"*[18] — one of those clear and concise expressions of which the Latin language is master. At first sight, it is a paradox, for a beginning is a beginning and then we go on. But that is true only in mechanical matters. In actual life, beginning is an element that must operate constantly. Nothing goes on if it does not at the same time begin.

So he who wishes to advance must always begin again. He must constantly immerse himself in the inner source of life and arise therefrom in new freedom, in initiative — the power of beginning — in order to make real what he has purposed: prudence, temperance, self-control, or whatever it may be that is to be accomplished.

Patience with oneself — not carelessness or weakness, of course, but the sense of reality — is the foundation of all progress.

Goethe's Faust, who was formerly the idol of the bourgeoisie, is impatient through and through; he is a dreamer who never grows up. He sells himself to magic, a way of expressing that he does not know how definitely the basis of all growth and accomplishment is formed by the acceptance of reality, endurance, and perseverance amid the things that are. Instead, he makes speeches, everything around him goes to pieces, and at the end there is a "redemption" which no one believes who understands what that word means.

---

[18]Literally, "Always begin"; *The Imitation of Christ* is a spiritual classic by ascetic writer Thomas à Kempis (c. 1380-1471).

When we were thinking about the concept of *virtue*, we noticed that there is no virtue which, if we will permit the old expression, is chemically pure. As in nature we do not find the pure tone, the pure color, but only refractions and chords, so there is no attitude which is pure patience, but many other elements must be mingled with it.

So, for example, patience is impossible without insight, without knowing the ways of life. Patience is wisdom, understanding what it means that I have this and not something else, that I am of this nature and not another, that the person with whom I am associated is as he is and not like another. I would like it to be different, and by persevering effort, I may be able to change many things, but basically things are as they are and I must accept that. Wisdom is insight into the way in which realization comes about: how an idea is lifted from the imagination and worked into the substance of existence. Wisdom is knowing how slow this process is and how greatly endangered, and how easily we may deceive ourselves and slip from our own hand.

Patience demands strength — great strength. The supreme patience rests upon omnipotence. Because God is the omnipotent, He can be patient with the world. Only the strong man can exercise living patience, can take upon himself again and again the things that are; only he can always begin anew. Patience without strength is mere passivity, dull acceptance, growing accustomed to being a mere thing.

Love, too, belongs to true patience — love of life. For living things grow slowly, take their time, and have many ways and turns. Life demands confidence, and only love can trust. He who does not love life has no patience with it. This leads to short circuits and to violence; and then there are wounds and destruction.

Many other things could be said on this subject.

Living patience is the whole man, standing in tension between what he would like to have and what he has, between what he ought to accomplish and what he is able at any given time to do, between what he wishes to be and what he really is. Working out this tension, again and again gathering things together in relation to the possibilities of the moment: that is patience. So we might say that patience is man in the process of becoming, with a true understanding of himself. And it is only in the hand of patience that those who are entrusted to us can thrive and grow. A father or mother who does not have patience, in this sense, will only harm the children. A teacher who does not have patience with those entrusted to him will frighten them and deprive them of sincerity.

When life has been placed in our hands, the work can prosper only if we carry it on with this deep and quiet power. It resembles the manner in which life itself grows. When we were children, we perhaps had a little garden, or just a flower-pot on the windowsill, and we planted seed. Was it not difficult to adapt ourselves to the way in which growth in the earth takes place? Did we not dig up the ground to see if the seed was growing — and then the germ perished? Did we not feel that growth was too slow, until the insignificant sprout appeared? And when the buds formed, did we not squeeze them to make them open? Instead, they turned brown and withered. The power under whose protection life can unfold is patience.

Again and again, we shall turn to the patience of the powerful one under whose protection we should grow, the living God. Woe to us if He were like Shiva, the impatient and foolish one; woe to us if He did not have the wisdom and long-suffering which, in quiet attention, holds the world, which He does not need but which He loves, permitting it to ripen.

Again and again, we shall turn to Him: "Lord, have patience with me, and give me patience so that the possibilities granted to me may, in the short span of my lifetime, those brief years, grow and bear fruit!"

Justice

Now we shall speak of justice. The word has a lofty but also a tragic sound. It has enkindled noble passion and inspired the practice of the finest generosity. But it also reminds us of great wrongs — of widespread destruction and suffering. The whole history of mankind could be recounted under the heading "The battle for justice."

In the Sermon on the Mount, in the Beatitudes,[19] the words of Jesus express the greatness and also the whole tragic quality of the matter concerned. He says, "Blessed are they that hunger and thirst after justice, for they shall have their fill."[20] The one who says this is no idealist remote from the world, but He of whom the Gospel says, "He knew what was in man."[21] Here He figuratively connects justice with that urge which determines the presence or absence of physical life — with hunger and thirst. In the heart of man — of the right-minded man, whom Jesus calls "blessed" — the desire for justice is as

[19]Matt. 5:3-11.
[20]Matt. 5:6.
[21]John 2:25.

elementary as hunger and thirst are in his physical life. How terrible is the lack when this desire is not fulfilled. But some-day — this is Christ's promise — it shall be satisfied.

By the word *justice*, Jesus means something which receives its full meaning only from Revelation: justification before God, the grace of pardon and sanctification.[22] But to bring home to us what that means, He connects the idea of salvation by God's grace with that of justice as the basic value of all moral existence and that of hunger and thirst for bodily satis-faction. So He suggests something elementary which concerns the whole man.

This basic and elementary thing shall now be the subject of our meditation.

We can speak of justice only in relation to man; it does not exist in the animal world. Where we seem to discern some-thing of the sort — perhaps in noble horses or highly bred dogs — it is a reflection of the human being in the animal which lives with him. Of its own nature, the animal knows nothing of justice, for it lacks what is central to justice: the person.

But what is a person? It is the manner in which man is man. A lifeless thing in nature exists as a thing, something without feeling, whose form, qualities, and energy are determined by the laws of nature. A living creature exists as an individual, a being that lives, grows from an inner center, maintains itself, unfolds, propagates, and dies. It, too, is determined by interior and exterior necessity. Man, however, exists as a person; that means he is not merely there, but he is conscious of himself.

[22]On this, see the final chapter, "Justice Before God."

He knows about himself; he is master of himself; he carries out his own work with judgment and in freedom. He stands not merely in a physical or biological relation to other persons, but converses with them and lives in a community which is established on a basis of intelligence.

The fact that man is a person gives to his existence the frightening seriousness and significance which we express by the words *conscience* and *responsibility*. Man not only exists, but his existence is committed to him, and he is accountable for the use he makes of it. He is not merely active; he *acts*, and he is responsible for his actions. This gives man dignity and honor. For this he desires freedom and a right order. He must desire them, inevitably, for the sake of spiritual self-preservation, for himself and for others, for mankind as such. This is, primarily, the desire for justice.

Justice, then, is that order in which man can exist as a person, in which he can form his judgment about himself and the world, can have a conviction which none can touch, and can be master of his decision and act according to his judgment. Justice is that order of existence in which man can participate in the world and carry on his work, and can form with other persons relationships of friendship, of association, and of love and fruitfulness according to the demands of his conscience. And, we must emphasize this again, this is true not only of one or another, not only of the powerful or fortunate or talented person, but of every man, because he is human.

The order which would guarantee this would be justice. But is there such a thing? Is not history really the tragedy of justice? Is it not a concatenation of the deeds by which

selfishness, violence, and falsehood have constantly endangered and destroyed this order? In any case, such an order
would be justice, and the man who desires it and strives for its
realization we call a just man.

Justice would go deeper if it determined destiny; if the man
who is good would in consequence be happy or if the man of
good disposition were successful, if the pure of heart were
always beautiful and the good man had a rich and full life; or
if, on the other hand, an evil disposition rendered its posses-
sor ugly, injustice brought misfortune, and every sin brought
vengeance upon the one who committed it — only upon him,
and never upon an innocent person.

This would be justice not merely in action, but in destiny.
But does it exist? Is it not the subject of fairy tales? Is this not
the reason why we — even as adults and with our experience
of life — never grow weary of these tales, whereas reality is so
completely different? In this deeper sense, the just man would
be the one who desired this state of affairs and did what he
could to bring it about, but he would also be Don Quixote,[23]
the dreamer who pursues the impossible and makes himself
ridiculous.

Perhaps the matter goes deeper still, and here we seem to
find something that we must call the "justice of being." This
is so improbable that one must almost fear to speak of it. We
surmise what it means if we listen to the complaints of human
hearts, complaints about its nonexistence: Why was I not born
strong and healthy instead of sickly? Why do I have these

---

[23]The chivalrous hero of Spanish novelist Miguel de Cervantes
Saavedra's (1547-1616) *Don Quixote de La Mancha*.

qualities and not others? Why do I not have the possibilities for which I envy my friend? And so on.

In the speech of all men, there appear questions which no wisdom can answer — those questions in which we find the word *why* and the word *I*. Why am I so? Why am I not so? Justice of being would exist if every man from the very first could agree to be as he is and who he is. But here we touch the basic mystery of ultimate being. The answer to these questions can be given only by God Himself; an answer which does not merely solve the problem but removes it in a living encounter.

But let us stay within the confines of everyday reality. How would it be if man strove for justice?

In regard to the existing order, he would do what he could to see that the laws of the land gave everyone his rights, that burdens were apportioned according to true capacity, that needs would be properly met, etc. These are great things, but let us disregard them for a moment. It often seems as if great things exist for the purpose of diverting people from those things that touch them seriously. Where does the justice of the existing order really become a serious matter? Here the answer would be less imposing but far more concrete. It would concern matters that touch our own life.

For example: if you spend ten dollars for yourself and later are supposed to do it for another, does the amount carry the same weight for you in both cases? Or do you say, or think or feel, in the first case, "only ten dollars," and in the second, "all of ten dollars"? Why the difference? It would be justice if you considered the amount as equivalent in both cases, for that would mean that another's need touched you as closely as your own. And even if there were a difference in the immediate feeling, yet your intention and action would be the same in both cases.

What is the situation in your home, in your family? Do you consider the different persons there of equal worth? Does an unkind word about one distress you as much as such a word spoken about another? Or do you like one person and become indignant about an injustice done to him, but think the matter not so serious if the injustice is done to another? Should not at least your practical conduct in both cases be the same?

Here, and not in the apportionment of taxes, does real justice begin: it begins at home, in our dealings with our friends, in the office, wherever we are associated with people. It consists in saying and giving and doing, as far as possible, that which the other has a right to expect.

And the justice of destiny, in which the life of man would be arranged as his disposition merits, how would this justice, insofar as we can speak of such a thing, appear in everyday life? What could one do who "hungers and thirsts" for it? He could not change much in the actual situation, for higher powers are in operation there; but he could, for example, make an effort to judge another not according to external appearances, but according to that person's intentions.

But how do we act in everyday matters? Do we give to those who live around us that first beginning of the justice of destiny, which consists in trying to understand what they mean? At home among our family or in business, when dealing with our associates, in short, among persons who are close to us, do we consider how somebody meant the word which offended us, why he was so irritated in a particular case, or what may have been the reason his work was so unsatisfactory?

Only in that way would we be dealing seriously with every-day reality; that is, not by attempting to establish a general culture of justice in which the interior and the exterior would correspond, but by giving to those persons with whom we are dealing a little of such justice.

The deepest stratum of justice is touched, as we saw, by the question concerning the differences of existence. Why are persons different in disposition? Why is one healthy and an-other an invalid? Why does one come from a harmonious family and another from a broken one? And so on through all the inequalities which press upon us everywhere. We cannot grasp their roots. Let us rather consider what would be possible in daily life.

There is, for example, the elementary question of whether we actually grant to the other the right to be as he is. If we consider the matter, we shall soon see that we usually do not do this at all, but, by aversion, ungraciousness, or bias, we reproach him for his own nature. But his existence gives him the right to be as he is; so we should grant it to him, and not only in theory, but also in our disposition and in our thoughts, in our daily attitude and actions. This we should do especially in our immediate environment, in our family, among our friends, associates, and colleagues. It would be justice to seek to understand the other person from his own point of view and to act accordingly. Instead we emphasize the injustice of exist-ence by sharpening and poisoning the differences through our judgment and actions.

But if things are so in the small circle which we can influence, how can they be otherwise in world affairs? Every-one should say to himself: "The history of nations moves in the same way as the affairs in my home. The state mirrors the way in which I order my small sphere of action." All criticism should begin with ourselves, and with the intention of improving things. Then we would soon see how much goes wrong because we do not permit the other person to be who he is and do not give him the room which he requires.

But will things never be properly ordered? If we put aside wishful thinking, we must reply: evidently not in the course of history. Of what avail are all the attempts to bring about justice on earth if we look not at ideologies and party politics but at reality — the whole reality?

Let us consider the present situation. Let us presume that those who live and fight today are really concerned about the establishment of justice; that is, a proper order of society, sufficient food for all, suitable working conditions for everyone, the possibility of education without special privileges, and so on. Then much would have been accomplished. But how much all this is intermingled with striving for power and self-will! How much injustice enters into it, how much falsehood, and even how much crime! Millions of persons are crushed in order that the supposedly correct form of economic conditions, of the social order, of government — even of justice — may be established. And let us assume that in all this, a forward step is taken. Does this take away and nullify all the terrible things which brought it about? Or is the evil still there, in the context of life, poisoning what has been attained?

A person is worthy of his humanity insofar as he strives to bring about justice in the place where he is; but as a whole, as that which it should be, as a condition of existence and an attitude of mankind, justice can never be attained. And here the idea of "progress," which has at present become a dogma, and the notion of the evolution of man beyond himself to ever greater heights must not confuse us. Personal experience, as well as history, tells another story. There is a basic disorder working in man which makes itself felt anew in everyone who is born.

Only by God will true and complete justice be established, and only through His judgment. We should try to let the revelation that this judgment will be passed upon all mankind affect us deeply. The first thing that everyone who thinks of the judgment should say to himself is, "Judgment will be passed upon me!" But there will also be a judgment upon all the human institutions and powers about which we are so likely to feel that they are sovereign and subject to no examination: the state, civilization, history.

The judgment must be taken into account in all being and action. It is God's verdict upon every finite reality. Without it everything is half-balanced in space. Only God determines it. He it is who sees through all, fearing nothing, bound by nothing, just in eternal truth. If a man does not believe in Him, his hunger and thirst shall never be satisfied.

Reverence

If one wishes to think about a phenomenon of human existence, it is well to notice the word by which language designates it, for language expresses more than the mind of the
individual. We wish to do this in dealing with the virtue upon
which we now intend to mediate, that is, reverence.[24]

It is a strange word, this combination of *fear* and *honor*: fear
which honors; honor which is pervaded by fear. What kind of
fear could that be? Certainly not the kind of fear that comes
upon us in the face of something that is harmful or causes pain.
That kind of fear causes us to defend ourselves or to seek safety.
The fear of which we shall speak does not fight or flee, but it
forbids obtrusiveness, keeps one at a distance, and does not
permit the breath of one's own being to touch the revered
object. Perhaps it would be better to speak of this fear as "awe."

This word leads us to an understanding of the phenomenon. The feeling of reverence has a religious origin. It is the
perception of the holy and unapproachable, which, in the

[24]The German word for *reverence*, *ehrfurcht*, combines the two
words *honor* and *fear*. The English word, from the Latin *vereor*,
also implies the idea of fear and respect. — TRANS.

experience of early man, surrounded all that was lofty, power-ful, and splendid. It included several things: a surmise of great-ness and holiness and a desire to participate in it, combined with the apprehension of being unworthy of it and of arousing a mysterious anger.

In the measure in which cultural evolution progressed, and a rational understanding and technical mastery of the world increased, the religious element receded. The concept of sig-nificance and value became predominant and awakened a respectful attitude in which there was still an echo of the old awe, that feeling of reverence of which we are speaking and by which a man of proper discernment still pays tribute to greatness.

In reverence, man refrains from doing what he usually likes to do, which is to take possession of and use something for his own purposes. Instead he steps back and keeps his distance. This creates a spiritual space in which that which deserves reverence can stand erect, detached, and free, in all its splendor. The more lofty an object, the more the feeling of value which it awakens is bound up with this keeping one's distance.

And yet the experience of value makes us wish to partici-pate in it. So we must determine more exactly for modern man why reverence steps back instead of pushing forward, why it removes its hands instead of grasping. Above all, the qualities of the person demand reverence: his dignity, freedom, and nobility. But also worthy of respect are the qualities of any work of man which reveal nobility or delicacy. And finally there is the phenomena of nature which express the sublime or mysterious.

Perhaps we can say that all true culture begins with the fact that man steps back. That he does not obtrude himself and seize hold of things, but leaves a space, so that there may be a place in which the person in his dignity, the work in its beauty, and nature in its symbolic power may be clearly discerned.

Reverence can also assume, so to speak, an everyday form. Every genuine virtue extends over many levels and stages because it is an attitude of a living person. Hence reverence can and should appear in everyday life, and then we call it "respect."

Respect is the most elementary thing that must be perceptible if people are to associate with each other as human beings. We need not consider particular values, talents, accomplishments, moral nobility, or the like, but simply the fact that the other person is a human being with freedom and responsibility.

So respect means that one takes another's conviction seriously. I may fight against it, for if I am of the opinion that what he says is wrong, then I have a right and, under certain circumstances, a duty to defend the truth as I see it. But I must do this with respect, conscious of the fact that I am dealing not with an abstract sentence in some book, but with a person, who, on the basis of his conscience, has decided upon this opinion. If I see that he is mistaken, I may contend with him, but I may not violate his opinion or wish to trick him by cunning.

Respect desires privacy for the other person, in the sphere of his own being and in connection with those among whom he lives and to whom he is related, his family and his friends. This is something which is increasingly forgotten in our day.

Everywhere we see the urge toward publicity; a mania to see just that which is reserved; a greed for sensation which finds an odious pleasure in unveiling, stripping, causing shame and confusion — and with this, the technique which renders it possible, the money behind newspapers, magazines, films, and television. What an atmosphere of disrespect for everything personal all this fosters!

How crude it is, for instance, to photograph a child who is praying, or a woman who is weeping because an accident has caused the death of her husband! The desire to strip what had previously been surrounded by reverence has actually glorified itself; it claims to be courage and frankness and speaks of "taboos" that must be destroyed. No one thinks of the destruction of security and sensitivity that is actually involved, or perhaps this is also desired and enjoyed.

On the other hand, how great is the desire to be publicized. For if the average reader of the illustrated paper had not the expressed or secret wish to see his own picture, then the force of public opinion would grow strong enough to abolish the whole show. Moreover, we must not forget how much this dwindling of respect, which shows itself in the destruction of privacy, prepares man for dictatorship. If a man no longer has a sphere reserved for himself, he is at the disposal of totalitarian usurpation.

We might point out many other things. Respect is the guarantee that the relations of one person to another preserve their dignity. If a friendship disintegrates, then the persons concerned may well ask themselves if there has not been a lack of respect. If a marriage goes bad and those who are bound by it no longer feel secure in each other, we are justified in assuming that they have treated each other like a piece of furniture (or worse, for furniture costs money).

Here we also find the root of what we call "courtesy." This does not signify something external. True courtesy is the expression of respect for the human person. It makes it possible that the many persons who constantly encounter each other in the limited space of life can do so without offending each other — in fact, even in such a way that the encounter is humanly valuable. We shall need to think about this point more carefully.

Respect is necessary wherever things human are concerned, either persons or works. But reverence awakens before what is great, the great personality and the great creation.

What is "greatness"? It is not something quantitative; not what we mean when we say, "The number one hundred is greater than the number ten." Rather, it is a manner of thinking and of meeting the world. It means the strictness of man's demands upon himself and the willingness to stand for what is important, a breadth of vision and boldness of decision, a depth of involvement, originality, and creative power.

It is not an easy thing to confront greatness. It can discourage, even paralyze, for the greatness of another makes me feel my own littleness. Goethe said that there is only one defense against great superiority, and that is love. I wonder if this is true. It may not always be possible to love. Perhaps it may be more correct to say that the defense against great superiority consists in truth and reverence, which say: "He is great, I am not. But it is good that greatness should be, even if it is not in me but in another." Then there is an open space, and envy disappears.

Learning the Virtues

The greatness of another, if one does not accept it honestly, awakens an anger which seeks to belittle it, a resentment. One begins to find fault, looks for imperfections in order to be able to say that what is praised is really not so worthwhile, maintains that it is just a matter of luck, and so on. If this succeeds, then everything becomes paltry, and we have debased the envied person.

But if one freely affirms and accepts the great man because greatness is beautiful, even if it is found in another, then a wonderful thing happens; at that moment, the one who reveres stands beside the one revered, for he has understood and recognized his greatness.

A similar reverence is demanded by a great work and a great deed. It is so important to encounter them, even if they cause our own accomplishments to shrink. I once asked a friend what culture really is. He answered: "Culture is the ability to judge. For in order to judge, we must have standards, which have become a vital part of our feelings: standards for great and small, genuine and false, noble and base."

To meet a great achievement wherever it may be, in scholarly research, poetic creation, the fine arts, or political action, and not to armor ourselves with the offended resentment of the man who wishes to achieve and is unable, but instead to open our mind and to recognize that it is good that someone had this ability — that is what gives us standards and enables us to judge.

We have seen that reverence is awakened in a well-ordered mind by a great person and a noble work, and that we can measure the degree of culture of a man by his ability to feel these and to respond freely and joyously to them. But it is strange, and an honor to man, that this feeling can also be aroused by what is small or defenseless, incapable of making its own way.

The low and vulgar man feels the impulse to exploit the defenselessness of the child, or the inexperienced or weak person; the decent man feels impelled to respect the defenseless. But why? It would seem a sensible thing to say that it is a matter of course for every right-feeling man to wish to help a child or a feeble person. Helpfulness, yes — but why reverence?

Perhaps it is because the decent man, when confronted by helplessness, is touched by the proximity of destiny and stops.

Then the matter takes on a religious meaning. We recall how Jesus speaks of children, and the "woe" that He pronounces upon those who harm the mind of a child[25] — a statement, by the way, that is generally forgotten today. How many are there who seriously concern themselves about such harm? How many are even conscious of the destructive impressions that those who are not yet morally capable of defending themselves can receive from magazines, radio, film, and television? Jesus says: Beware, "for their angels always behold the face of my Father who is in Heaven."[26] Behind the defenselessness of the child stands the watchfulness of the angel who beholds the holiness of God. And what holds true of the child holds true of all who are defenseless.

These are profound matters which we should take to heart.

The right-minded man feels reverence before a great personality or a great work, but also before the defenseless person,

[25]Matt. 18:6-7.
[26]Matt. 18:10.

the inexperienced, the weak, the suffering, and the afflicted. It is a sign of increasing barbarism if misfortune is manhandled and turned into a sensation in illustrated papers and magazines. The decent man feels sorrow for human suffering and respects the privacy of those involved. Beware that they may not take vengeance upon you in the coarsening of your feelings, and also that similar misfortunes may not befall you as well.

Ultimately, however, all reverence culminates in reverence for the holy.

We feel it when we enter a church. Churches are built in such lofty and impressive style that, even as we enter, the space affects us. If this does not happen, then it is not, in essence, a church that we see, but merely an assembly hall. For this reason, we step softly in a church and speak in a low tone. How the barbarism of our time is revealed when travelers in a church behave as if they were in a museum or a stadium!

But there is something even worse: the holy provokes the rebellious spirit in man, drives him to mockery, to blasphemy, and to violence. Half the world is full of this. Such feelings and dispositions have made atheism a political power. And let no one say that he is a stranger to them; actually, they lurk in everyone in consequence of the primeval rebellion. So it is well if we keep alive the feeling of reverence toward the holy.

The basic act of this reverence is the adoration of God. It expresses the true nature of man most perfectly, especially if the body also performs the act in bowing. It must give us pause to note that this attitude is so very inconspicuous in religious life. Usually we find only petition or thanks, and less frequently, praise; adoration scarcely ever appears. And yet it is so essential. "I adore God" means I am aware that He is and that I stand before Him; that He is the one who essentially is, the Creator, and that I am His creature; that He is holy and I am not, and that I adapt myself with heart and mind to the Holy One who confronts me. Adoration is truth in act.

And now we shall go a step farther. We have constantly tried to carry the virtue which we are considering even into God Himself, because "the good" is ultimately the One who is good. He alone is good, as Jesus said to the young man,[27] and all that is good in man is an element of the divine image. How does this apply? Does God Himself show reverence?

We certainly do not wish to talk nonsense, but I believe that we must answer this question in the affirmative. The reverence is revealed in the fact that God created man as a free being. We often encounter a kind of humility which, in order to honor God, debases man. This is not Christian. It is fundamentally the converse of the idolizing of man, and converse attitudes tend to interchange.

God wishes man to be His image; that is, possessing knowledge and responsibility. This expresses a divine will to reverence, for God might have created man so that he would be bound to the good. This would imply nothing base — perhaps even, if we think of the horrible flood of evil and crime which inundates the world, something great and blissful. He might have permitted His truth, even from the beginning, to send its beams so powerfully into the mind of man, might have set up the nobility of the good so basically in man's conscience that it would have been quite impossible for man to err or to sin.

[27]Mark 10:18; Luke 18:19.

Then the world would have been a work of art, beautiful and harmonious, but the wonderful fact of a free creature would have been lacking, and also God's attitude toward this freedom, which we can only express by saying that God reverences man. This brings about the holy world of the kingdom of God, which grows, by His grace, out of the freedom of man.

This also throws a new light upon another basic truth of Revelation, the event which concludes the whole of history and fixes man's destiny for all eternity: the judgment. When one speaks of this, it is usually as of something dreadful. In reality, the judgment is a testimony of honor for man, for it places him in a position of responsibility. Only a free and responsible being can be judged.

Here a mystery prevails which no one can fathom. God's will is the basis of all being and action, and yet man is free. He is truly free, so much so that he can even say no to God's will. But this freedom does not exist beside the will of God; even less is it an opposing power rising up against Him, but it is God Himself through whom it exists and operates — His reverence.

The reverence of God for freedom and at the same time the decisiveness with which He wills the good and only the good: perhaps nothing has been reflected upon as much as this mystery, but no one as yet has penetrated it.

Is it possible to reach even greater depths?

God is the Absolutely Existent One, self-based and self-sufficient. How can anything finite exist "beside" Him or "before" Him, especially finite freedom? Must He not, as the only existent one, rise up in the triumph of His absoluteness? You may reply, "That would be the icy triumph of eternal loneliness!" But Revelation tells us that He, the Triune God, possesses within Himself unending community, incomprehensible fruitfulness; that He is Father and Son and Holy Spirit, speaker and spoken and, in infinite love, comprehending and comprehended. It is a mystery, certainly, impenetrable for our minds, but revealing to us that He does not need the finite in any way, not in order to attain consciousness or to gain love, as the pride of pantheism maintained.

And yet He wills that the finite should exist and should be free. Does this not reveal a mystery of divine reverence: that the absolute power of the divine act of being does not crush the finite being; the glowing majesty of the divine "I" — no, "We"[28] — does not consume the finite but, on the contrary, wills it, creates it by a never-ending call, and preserves it in its reality?

Truly "in Him we live and move and are," as St. Paul said on the Areopagus in Athens.[29] His creative reverence is the "space" in which we exist. In our day, when that terrible mixture of arrogance and folly which is called "atheism" is flooding the world, it is good to think of that truth.

[28] Cf. John 14:23.
[29] Acts 17:28.

Loyalty

If, in the following pages, we are to deal with loyalty, then it is essential that we call to mind the connotations of the word at the present time. Generally, we avoid using the word *loyalty*. Like many another word expressing moral values, it no longer sounds quite genuine to us. It seems too great, too lofty, and, in the face of the confused reality of our life, too simple.

Many factors have contributed to this thinking: poetic bombast, official rhetoric, and the dishonesty of politicians and newspapermen. Likewise, equally important is the fact that, during years of terror, an absolute and unconditional adherence, a readiness for every sacrifice was demanded of us, something which no earthly cause has the right to demand, while at the same time, the very persons who demanded this betrayed us in most hideous fashion.[30]

Nevertheless, it remains true that our life rests upon loyalty. So it is well to consider carefully what this worn-out word means.

[30]The author is alluding particularly to life in Germany under the Nazi government. — ED.

Learning the Virtues

First of all, we must understand clearly that the word is applied to two different ways of behavior. The one is a psychological disposition. In a person of this type, psychic processes are slow but go very deep. Feelings are strong. They do not flare up quickly and then die out, but they continue and bring about an enduring state of mind. Decisions are formed slowly, but they remain as an interior direction and can be relied upon to determine action. When a person of this type bestows his affections upon another or determines to support him, the bond is solid and survives every kind of vicissitude. These are fine qualities, although they also have their dark side, the danger of rigidity, narrowness, and injustice. But, as we have said, they are a matter of natural disposition which we cannot bestow upon ourselves and cannot ethically demand of another.

Other natures are different, but they also are obliged to practice loyalty. In their case, it is not supported by a particular psychic structure, but must depend upon a basis which can be presupposed in everyone. That is the human person with his insight into true and false, right and wrong, honor and dishonesty, the freedom of decision and the firmness with which this decision is maintained for the sake of the other person and his confidence, and for the sake of the choice that has been made. Or, if the decision threatens to waver, it is renewed and reaffirmed again and again.

What is the meaning of this virtue? We may describe it as a force which conquers time, that is, change and transition — not with the hardness of a stone, in rigid motionlessness, but living, growing, and creative. Let us try to imagine it.

Two persons have met, have fallen in love, and decide to marry. This relationship is at first supported by the desire of the one vitality for the other, feelings of congeniality, common experiences, harmony in relation to nature and men, similar preferences and inclinations, and so forth.

These feelings at first seem to guarantee a life-long bond. But they can easily cease. Differences, such as we always find between different persons, appear. And now is the time for true loyalty: each of the two must be aware that the other trusts him, depends upon him, that they have formed a bond which determines their life, that this must be supported by what is best in them, the core of their humanity, the person and his dependability. And now self-conquest begins: to stand by the other and keep him — not in order to possess and dominate, but to preserve the life that rests upon the bond and to bring it to full fruition and unfolding; to know that one is responsible for the other; not to prescribe to him what he should be, but to give him freedom to be what he truly is, to help him to become what his nature meant him to be; to accept him again and again and stand at his side.

We must consider, too, that when two persons come together, each one comes with a definite character. But "to live" means to grow and consequently to change. Some characteristics show themselves in childhood, others in adolescence, and others in later years. So it can happen that on some occasion, the one person says to the other in consternation, "I just don't know you anymore! You were not like this when I began to love you." It may be that the person feels abandoned, even deceived, as if the other had disguised himself, whereas it was actually only a living development that revealed his new qualities. Again this is the time for loyalty, so that the change may be surmounted and the relationship may endure. And this must be done not in rigidity and constraint, but in such a way that the one receives the other again and again and accommodates himself to the other. All this can be difficult — under certain circumstances, very difficult. The disappointed feelings may rebel. But to the extent to which this loyalty is practiced, it grows deeper and brings about what truly constitutes a marriage.

Let us continue our reflection: loyalty means remaining true to a responsibility in spite of loss or danger.

For example, one has assumed certain obligations. He has thought over the matter carefully, recognized it as proper, and the other person depends upon his decision. But now the circumstances change and losses threaten. Loyalty means that he keeps his word and assumes the losses, as he would expect the other person to do if the situation were reversed.

Or a person is seized by an idea, recognizes the necessity of an action, and commits himself to it. As might be expected, difficulties arise. Loyalty means that he stands firm and fights on. Or it may be a case of dangers resulting from one's profession. A physician feels that his work is wearing out his strength, perhaps threatening his life. A civil servant has a difficult post, perhaps especially difficult because others take it easy. Loyalty says, "Hold on!"

And what is this really which we call "conviction"? First of all, it is insight. One has seen that something is so, and then the thing is certain. It does not require any further support — for example, that it coincides with the opinions of the age, or brings advantages, or anything of the sort. But wherever persons are concerned, mere logical reasons are not sufficient; the decision must be based upon a personal obligation. The strength with which this cleaves to what has been accepted and affirmed, even in times and situations in which the reasons seem pale and uncertain, is loyalty.

Loyalty overcomes change, injury, and danger, but not by a power of persistence inherent in one's disposition. That may exist, and happy is the one who possesses it. But loyalty is more than that; it is the firmness which results when a man has assumed a responsibility and abides by it. This quality overcomes the variability, the injuries, and the dangers of life by the power of conscience.

A person of this sort can be trusted. We feel that in him there is a point which is beyond fear and weakness, and which gives him ever-renewed strength to persevere in his resolve.

But we must not forget another loyalty; that is, loyalty to God. What happens when a man, in a mature decision, resolves to believe? At first he is influenced by all that he has learned from his parents, from the atmosphere of his home, from his teachers, from the life of the Church, and from other sources.

He himself may have had religious experiences. In a moment of heartfelt prayer, he may have sensed something that was holy and loving and that supported him. Or he may have experienced on certain occasions what *Providence* means. The answers of the Christian religion to the problems of existence have convinced him. He noticed that if he followed its counsels, he became better, more resolute, more possessed of interior resources, and the like. Thereupon he made his decision and gave God his faith. This first faith is fine, generous, and filled with the consciousness of profound meaning. But in time, these feelings may change or even disappear.

Perhaps the feeling of God's nearness vanishes, and the believer seems to be standing in a religious vacuum. Or he experiences how much of human weakness inheres in the religious world. Or events take place which he cannot harmonize with the concept of Providence. Or the views of the contemporary world move away from faith and make it seem antiquated. Then faith loses the support of feeling, of its environment, and of the circumstances and events of life, and the doctrines of revelation which at first seemed so wonderfully clear, grow pale. Then the question may arise in his mind whether he has not been mistaken, whether he has not been the victim of some idealistic illusion.

At such moments, one may feel very foolish in holding on to faith. But this is the time for loyalty, which says, "I will remain firm. When I first believed, it was not a mere inclination of feeling or the attraction of a beautiful idea that became effective; rather, it was an act of the core of the personality, in all seriousness. The word *faith* implies a promise — a promise of loyalty. God relies upon this promise; therefore I cling to Him."

In this way, *faith* acquires a new meaning; it is the act by which man endures through the period of God's silence and absence. When God lets us feel His nearness, when His word comes to life, then it is not difficult to be sure of His reality; it is joy. But when He conceals Himself, when we feel nothing and the sacred word is silent, then it becomes difficult. But this is the time for true faith.

Loyalty is something that outlasts the flow of time. It has within it something of eternity. And since we are speaking of eternity: what of God Himself? Does the word *loyalty* have any meaning in His case? This question leads us to profound matters; let us take them to heart very carefully.

When God created the world, He gave it true greatness. The scientific researches of the last decades have brought this to our attention in overpowering fashion: greatness in magnitude and, if we may say so, greatness in the minute. Our thought is staggered by what has been revealed.

The world is greater than we can conceive. But compared with God, it is small, for He is absolute. We cannot use the word *is* of God and of the world in the same sense. We cannot say that God and the world "are." He *is* absolutely — glorious in Himself and self-sufficing. The world is through Him, before Him, and in reference to Him. But when He created it, He did not do so in sport, but in divine seriousness. He staked His honor upon it. He gave it — I think we may rightly say this — His loyalty, when He said it was "good." We read this six times in the first account of the creation and, at the end, a seventh time: "God saw all that He had created and behold, it was very good."[31] In this way, He bound Himself to the world.

We have already spoken of the Indian myth in which the god Shiva produced the world in an exuberance of creative joy and then grew weary of it, shattered it, and made a new one and after that another one, and so on. This would be the image of a god who was not loyal to his work. His demands would always be frustrated by the finiteness of the world. After a while, he would find it unsatisfactory, and he would discard it. It would be terrible to be in the hands of such a god.

[31]Gen. 1:31.

But the God who has revealed Himself to us is not like that. He holds fast to His work; He keeps the world in being. It exists each moment as a result of His loyalty.

This was, if we may say so, the "test" of God's loyalty to the world which lies in the very finiteness of all that is created, a quality that can never be abolished. But there was another test, which should never have taken place. It came not from the nature of things but from history, from man's freedom, from a misuse of this freedom, and from revolt; and it constantly springs forth again from man's rebellion. Now the loyalty of God becomes a basic principle of Revelation.

Sacred Scripture tells us how God, in order to bring about redemption, called a nation and entered into a covenant with it, which rested wholly upon His eternal loyalty. Out of this covenant, which again and again stood the test of man's unfaithfulness, grew the history of the Old Testament. Finally God's loyalty accomplished the inconceivable, taking upon Himself the responsibility for man's guilt, stepping into history by the Incarnation, and so accepting a destiny.

The life of Jesus is one entire expression of loyalty. This is shown by the way in which He persevered in remaining in narrow, hostile Palestine, because He knew that He had been sent as a party to the covenant of Sinai, even though the wide pagan world would readily receive Him. He persevered even to death — and what a death!

It is from God that loyalty comes into the world. We can be loyal only because He is so, and because He has willed us, who are made in His image, to be loyal also.

Disinterestedness

Perhaps this title surprises the reader, for who is likely, at present, to consider disinterestedness a virtue; that is, an example of moral value?

There is a proverb which comes from ancient China and which states that the fewer interests a man has, the more powerful he is; that the greatest power is complete disinterestedness. But that idea is foreign to us. The image of man which has become the standard since the middle of the past century is quite different. It presents the active man who moves with decision in dealing with the world and accomplishes his purposes. This man has many interests and considers himself perfect when everything that he does is subordinated to the goals that he sets up for himself.

That such a man accomplishes much would not be denied even by the teachers of that ancient philosophy. But they would probably say that most of it is superficial and bypasses that which is really important.

How, then, does the man live who is ruled by his interests?

In his associations with others, such a man does not turn toward another person with simplicity and sincerity, but he always has ulterior motives. He wishes to make an impression, to be envied, to gain an advantage, or to get ahead. He praises in order to be praised. He renders a service in order to be able to exact one in return. Therefore he does not really see the other as a person; instead, he sees wealth or social position, and then there is always rivalry.

With such a man we are not at ease. We must be cautious. We perceive his intentions and draw back. The free association in which true human relations are realized does not develop. Of course, our life with its many needs also has its rights. Many human relations are built upon dependence and aims. Consequently, it is not only right but absolutely necessary that we should seek to obtain what we need and should be conscious of doing this. But there are many other relations which rest upon a candid and sincere meeting of persons. If interests and ulterior motives determine our attitude in such cases, then everything becomes false and insincere.

Wherever the essential relations of "I" and "thou" are to be realized, interests must give way. We must see the other as he is, deal simply with him, and live with him. We must adapt ourselves to the situation and its demands, whether it be a conversation, collaboration, joyfulness, or the enduring of misfortune, danger, or sorrow.

Only in this way are true human values made possible, such as a real friendship, true love, sincere comradeship in working, and honest assistance in time of need. But if interests become dominant here, then everything atrophies.

A man who keeps interests in their proper place acquires power over others, but it is a peculiar kind of power. Here we approach the ancient aphorism of which we spoke in the beginning. The more we seek to gain our own ends, the more the other person closes up and is put on the defensive. But the more clearly he perceives that we do not wish to drive him, but simply to be with him and live with him — that we do not want to gain something from him, but merely to serve the matter at hand — then the more quickly he discards his defenses and opens himself to the influence of our personality.

The power of personality becomes stronger in proportion to the absence of interests. It is something quite different from that energy by which a man subordinates another to his will, and which is really a very external thing in spite of its dynamic quality. The power of personality stems from the genuineness of life, the truth of thought, the pure will to work, and the sincerity of one's disposition.

Something similar holds true of a man's relation to his work. When a man who is dominated by his interests works, then his work lacks precisely that which gives it value; that is, a sincere service to the thing itself. For him the first and chief consideration is how he can get ahead and further his career. He knows very little of the freedom of work and the joy of creation.

If he is a student, he works only with an eye to his vocation, and very frequently not even to that which really deserves the name of vocation, which is a man's feeling that he is "called" to a certain task within the context of human society. Rather, he works with an eye to that which offers the most opportunities for financial gain and for prestige. He really works only for the examination; he learns what is required and what the professor in each case demands. We must not exaggerate; these things, too, have their rights. But if they are the sole motives, then the essential thing is lost. That kind of student never has the experience of living in the milieu of knowledge, of feeling its freedom and its greatness. He is never touched by wisdom and understanding; his interests isolate him. What we have said of students also holds true of other forms of preparation for later life.

Naturally, we repeat, these other things have their rights. A man must know what he wants; otherwise his actions disintegrate. He must have a goal and must orient his life to that goal. But the goal should lie mainly in the object to which be devotes himself. He will pay attention to remuneration and advancement, since his work gives him the means of which he and his family have need and gives him wealth and the esteem of others. But the real and essential consideration must always be what the work itself demands, that it be done well and in its entirety.

The man who has this attitude will not let his actions be determined by considerations extrinsic to the task. In this sense, he is disinterested. He serves, in the fine sense of the word. He does the work which is important and timely; he is devoted to it and does it as it should be done. He lives in it and with it, without self-interest or side glances.

This is an attitude that seems to be disappearing in most places. Persons who do their duty in sincere devotion, because the work is valuable and fine, seem to be becoming rare. Actions are increasingly based upon utilitarian motives and considerations of success apart from the real matter in hand. And yet disinterestedness is the only disposition which pro-duces the genuine work, the pure act, because it frees man for creativity. It alone gives rise to what is great and liberating, and only the man who works in this way gains interior riches.

Disinterestedness

What we have said also opens the way to the final essence of humanity — selflessness. One of the most profound para-doxes of life is the fact that a man becomes more fully himself the less he thinks of himself. To be more precise, within us there lives a false self and a true self. The false self is the constantly emphasized "I" and "me" and "mine," and it refers everything to its own honor and prosperity, wishing to enjoy and achieve and dominate. This self hides the true self, the truth of the person. To the extent that the false self disappears, the true self is freed. To the extent that a man departs from himself in selflessness, he grows into the essential self. This true self does not regard itself, but it is there. It experiences itself, but in the consciousness of an interior freedom, sincer-ity, and integrity.

The way in which a man puts away the false self and grows into the real self is that which the masters of the interior life call "detachment." The saint is the person in whom the false self has been wholly conquered and the true self set free. Then the person is simply there without stressing himself. He is powerful without exertion. He no longer has desires or fears. He radiates. About him, things assume their truth and order.

Shall we say, with reference to essentials, that that man has opened himself for God, has become, if we may use the term, penetrable for God? He is the "door" through which God's power can stream into the world and can create truth and order and peace.

There is an event which reveals this marvel. When St. Francis[32] had lived through the long loneliness on Mount La

[32]St. Francis of Assisi (1182-1226), founder of the Franciscan Order.

Verna and had received the stigmata of Christ's Passion in his hands, feet, and side and returned to his people, they came and kissed the wounds in his hands. Francis, so basically humble, would have, in former times, rejected with horror these marks of reverence. Now he permitted them, for he no longer felt that he, "the son of Bernardone of Assisi" was their object, but Christ's love in him was. His exterior self had been quenched, but the real Francis shone — he who no longer stood in his own light, but was wholly transparent for God.

Every genuine virtue, as we have seen before, not only pervades the whole of human existence, but it reaches beyond it to God. More correctly, it comes down from God to man, for its true and original place is the divine life. How does this apply in the case of disinterestedness? Does not God have interests — He, through whose will everything exists and whose wisdom orders all things?

We must be careful not to confuse meanings. To "have interests," in the sense in which we have used the term, means something other than being active. Every activity has a goal, an end to be attained; otherwise, there would be chaos. In this sense, God looks toward the goal He has set, and directs His activity toward it. It is a different thing when the person acting is not simply looking toward the other person or the work to be accomplished, but regards himself, wishes to be recognized, and to secure an advantage. How could God intend anything of the sort? He is the Lord, Lord of the world, Lord of the divine life and existence. What could He need? He has — no, He is — everything!

When He creates the world, He does not do so as a man would make something, in order to boast of it or to serve his own needs, but He creates through pure, divine joy in the act. We may use the term *joy* here, in its highest sense. He creates things so that they may exist, that they may be truthful, genuine, and beautiful. We cannot conceive of the freedom and joyfulness of God's creative activity.

But what of the government of the world, that which we call "Providence"? Doesn't God have purposes? Doesn't He guide man, every man, and all the events of his life, to the end that He has proposed? Isn't the life of one man arranged in a certain way because the life of another is connected with it in this manner? Aren't the lives of all men oriented toward each other, and isn't the whole of existence arranged by divine wisdom according to God's plan?

Again, we must distinguish the meanings of words. Supreme wisdom does not will "interests" which accompany and are extrinsic to the essential thing, but the very meaning of that which is willed, its truth, and the fulfillment of its nature.

This divine will is the power which binds one thing to another, refers one event to another, brings one person into relation with another, and brings every man into relation with the whole. This does not constitute interests, but wisdom, the sovereign wisdom of the perfect Master who creates human existence as a woven fabric in which every thread supports all the others and is itself supported by all the others.

At present, we do not yet see the pattern. We see only the reverse of the tapestry and are able to follow certain lines for a short distance, but then they disappear. But someday the tapestry will be turned, at the end of time, at the Final Judgment; then the figures will stand out brightly. Then the question never fully answered (or not answered at all) in the course of time — "Why": Why this sorrow? Why this privation? Why can one do this and not another? — and all the questions of life's trials will receive their answer from the wisdom of God, which brings it about that things are not a mere mass of objects and events, are not a confusion of occurrences, but that all these together constitute a world.

Asceticism

There was a time when people spoke not only scornfully but with annoyance about anything that can be called "asceticism," as if it were not merely something wrong, but something unnatural and insulting. They thought that asceticism arose from the fear and hatred of life, even from perverted feelings; that it revealed the hatred of Christianity for the world, the corrupted sentiments of the priest who depreciated living nature in order to justify his own existence, and so on.

That was the time of liberal bourgeois prosperity. Things seem to have changed somewhat since then. Nevertheless the word *asceticism* still awakens resentment, so it is worthwhile to ask what it really means.

Much of the resistance against asceticism stemmed from the desire for license in following one's urges and instincts. But this also involved a false concept of life, or, more exactly, of the manner in which life grows and bears fruit.

How does life function in nature? Men like to compare man with nature when they wish to make room for something which is contrary to the spirit of Christ. How does life go on in nature? How does a healthy animal grow and develop? By following its urges. Then everything turns out well, for in-stinct keeps it from going wrong. If an animal is satisfied, it stops eating. If it is rested, it gets up. When the urge toward procreation is active, the animal follows it. When the time has passed, the urge is silent. The manner, the type, so to speak, according to which the life of nature is carried on is simply that of working out its fulfillment. The interior drive expresses itself in external action.

But what is the case with man? In him, there is a force at work which we do not find in the animal. This is so plainly real and operative that one must be blind in order not to see it. It is the spirit. This brings all that we call nature into a new situation.

In the realm of the spirit, the urge has a different meaning than it has in mere nature. It plays and works differently; so it is foolish to seek to understand the life of man by comparing it with the life of the animal. At present, men often carry the folly to greater lengths and try to understand man by compar-ing him with a machine. But let us not go into that. In any case, it is foolish to set up the life of an animal as the measure of the life of man.

What is the function of the spirit in regard to human urges: in the drive toward food, procreation, activity, rest, and com-fort? First of all, something surprising: it intensifies the urge. No animal follows the drive toward food as much as a man who makes the pleasure its own end and thereby harms him-self. In no animal does the sexual urge reach the boundless extent which it has in a man who permits it to destroy his honor and his life. No animal has the urge to kill that man has. His wars have no real counterpart in the animal kingdom.

All that we can call an urge operates differently in a man than in an animal. The spirit gives a unique freedom to the life-impulses; they become stronger and deeper, with far greater possibilities of demand and response. But at the same time, they lose the protection of the organic order which binds and secures them in the animal. They become unregulated, and their meaning is endangered.

The concept of "living to the limit" is a blind one. The animal lives to the limit; it must. But man must not. The spirit gives a new meaning to the urge. It works into the urge and gives it depth, character, and beauty. It brings it into relation with the world of values, and also with that which bears these values — the person — and so lifts it to the sphere of freedom. In the animal, the drives constitute "nature"; the spirit makes of them what we call "culture," taking this word as an expression of responsibility and self-conquest.

In the case of the animal, the drive builds the environment that is suited to its kind, but thereby also accommodates it to conditions and limitations. In the case of man, it leads to a free encounter with the breadth and wealth of the world, but thereby it is also endangered. All that we call excessive, overwrought, and unnatural becomes possible — and enticing.

The spirit elevates man above the urge, not thereby destroying it or becoming, as a foolish statement expresses it, the "adversary of life." Only a corrupt spirit, traitor to its own nature, does that. By the spirit, man acquires the possibility of ordering and forming the urge, and so leading it to greater heights, to its own perfection, even as an urge. Of course, it is thereby exposed to the danger of deformation and of going counter to nature.

Let us emphasize once more that all this points to the fact that a drive or urge in man means something different from an urge in the animal and that it makes no sense if a man seeks the pattern for his life in the animal or in mere nature. Asceticism means that a man resolves to live as a man.

This brings about a necessity which does not exist for the animal; that is, the need to keep his urges in an order which is freely willed and to overcome his tendency toward excess or toward a wrong direction.

This is not to imply that the urges are in themselves evil. They belong to the nature of man, and operate in all forms and areas of his life. They compose his store of energy. To weaken them would be to weaken life. But life is good. A deep current in the history of religion and ethics proceeds from the thought that the urges as such, sexual activity, the body, and even matter itself are evil — indeed the very principle of evil — while the spirit as such is good. This is dualism, in which, certainly, noble motives are at work; but, as a whole, it becomes a dangerous error, and very often ends in a surrender to the urge.

The motive for true asceticism does not lie in such a struggle to overcome the urges, but in the necessity of bringing them into proper order. The order is determined by various considerations: the question of health, regard for other persons, and our duties to our vocation and our work. Every day makes new demands and obliges us to keep ourselves in order. And this is asceticism. The word, derived from the Greek *áskesis*, means practice and exercise, exercise in the proper directing of one's life.

We must also consider the fact that there is a hierarchy of values. For instance, there are everyday values: those that pertain to our physical life; above these there are the values of our vocation and our work; still higher are those of personal relations and intellectual activity; and finally those which are attained by our immediate relation to God. We realize these values by means of the powers of our being; but these are limited, and we must understand clearly to which tasks we want to turn them. We must choose, and then carry out our choice. This requires exertion and sacrifices — and that, too, is asceticism.

Apart from all this, everyone who knows the tendency of human nature toward self-indulgence also knows how necessary it is to impose upon ourselves voluntary exercises in self-control, such as are not demanded by our immediate purposes. They are necessary so that the will may more easily fulfill the demands of duty when these present themselves. They are necessary also as a way to freedom which consists in being master of oneself, of one's impulses and circumstances.

The physical urges which proceed from the somatopsychic organization of man present themselves so plainly to our consciousness that the mental and spiritual urges can easily be overlooked. But these, as a matter of fact, are more decisive from the point of view of our total community life. The building up of what we call "the personality," its preservation in the world, and its activity and creativity is based upon mental and spiritual urges. There is the urge toward recognition and esteem, toward power in all its forms. There is the urge toward social and community life, toward freedom and culture, toward knowledge and artistic creation, etc. All of these urges have, as we said, their significance as impulses basic to self-preservation and self-development. But they are also inclined to become excessive, to bring our life out of harmony with the lives of others and so to become disturbing or destructive.

Therefore a constant discipline is necessary, a discipline whose principles are determined by ethics and practical philosophy; this discipline is asceticism.

But let us put aside generalities and look at a concrete situation — for example, a friendship. Two persons have learned to know and like each other. They have discovered a community of tastes and viewpoints. They find each other congenial and trust each other. They think that their friendship is secure and make no further efforts to preserve it. But, as we can expect, there are also differences between them, and gradually these make themselves felt. Misunderstandings arise — annoyances, tensions. But neither of the two seeks the causes where they really are, namely in his own self-confidence and carelessness, and after a short time, the two get on each other's nerves. The quiet confidence disappears, and gradually the whole relationship disintegrates.

If a friendship is to endure, it must be guarded. There must be something that will preserve it. Each of the two must give the other room to be what he *is*. Each must become conscious of his own failings and regard those of the other with the eyes of friendship. To will this and to carry it out in the face of the hypersensitiveness, sloth, and narrowness of our own nature — that again is asceticism.

Why do so many marriages grow dull and empty? Because each of the two partners has the basic idea that the purpose of marriage is "happiness," which means that each can find fulfillment in simply living his own life to the fullest extent.

Actually, a true marriage is a union of two lives; it is helpfulness and loyalty. Marriage means that "each shall bear the other's burden," as St. Paul says.[33] So a spiritual responsibility must keep watch over it. Again and again, each must accept the other as the person he is, must renounce what cannot be, must put away the mendacious notions fostered by films, which destroy the reality of marriage. He must know that after the finding of each other in the first stage of love, the task just begins. A genuine marriage can endure only through self-discipline and self-conquest. Then it becomes real, capable of producing life and of sending life into the world.

Someone founds an institution, undertakes a work, or does whatever his vocation entails. Let us imagine the most propitious case, that this is his true vocation and he is doing that for which he has talent or ability, and so likes doing it. At first he enjoys the task and puts forth every effort.

Perhaps it would be necessary even then to tell him to keep within the measure of the possible and not to overdo. For after a time, the tension relaxes, the more quickly as the original effort was more intense; but the tasks continue. What will happen if they are based only on the "full life," the joy in working and in accomplishing results? Then indifference will result and later aversion, and finally everything will collapse.

No work can flourish if it is not sustained by a responsibility which induces a man to perform his task faithfully and unselfishly.

Human life has many strata. There are superficial things, some that go deeper, and some that are quite essential — and

[33]Cf. Gal. 6:2.

each stratum has its requirements, values, and fulfillments. Plainly, we cannot have everything at the same time; we must choose, must surrender one thing in order that the other can come to pass.

Let us consider everyday life once more. The man who constantly watches movies loses his taste for great drama; he no longer understands it. So he must ask himself what he really wants and must choose. He must put away the superficial charms of the movies in order to be capable of experiencing what is more valuable, perhaps to become so once more; or he must stay with the movies and persuade himself that these are the art of the times, that he needs the relaxation, and cannot force himself, after the toil of the day, to the mental exertion that real drama demands, and so on.

The person who reads a great deal of trash loses the taste for good reading. So he must make up his mind as to what is more important for him. One who is constantly among people, talking and discussing, loses the ability to live with himself, and so loses all that which only reveals itself in solitude. Again it is a question of either-or. And much self-control is required to triumph over the restlessness which drives one out.

If a man wishes to obtain from life the precious gifts that it can bestow, then he must know that it is only by renouncing a lesser good that he can have the greater.

The people who preach the gospel of the "good life" say that we must not curtail this life; we must bring out all its possibilities and enjoy them. If we ask them what the true content of this life — its meaning and its standard — may be, they answer, "Life itself, the strong, sensitive rich life." But is that true? Is life its own meaning and measure?

Not only ordinary people speak in this way. There have been whole philosophies that have taught the same thing. But is it not very revealing that today we have the opposite of this — namely, a philosophy of disappointment and of nausea?

The meaning of life does not consist in enjoying one's own sensations and powers, but in bringing about the fulfillment of the task assigned to us. Man lives truly and fully if he knows his responsibility; if he carries out the task that awaits him; and if he meets the needs of the persons entrusted to him. But to recognize and to choose the right thing and reject what is wrong — this constant effort to transcend one's own wishes and meet one's obligations — that is asceticism.

Let us finally consider that which determines the meaning of our existence, the relation to the one who created us, under whose glance we live and before whom we must appear after our few years upon earth; then we shall easily see that no relation to Him can be established without discipline and self-conquest.

Man is not driven forcibly to God. If he does not discipline himself, betake himself to prayer in the morning and in the evening, make the observance of the Lord's Day an important occasion, and have a book at hand which will show him again and again something of the "breadth and length and height and depth" of the things of God,[34] then his life continually passes over the quiet admonitions that come from within. When he should be with God, he is bored, for everything seems empty. Lectures, newspapers, and radio teach him that religious values and relationships do not exist any longer for

[34]Eph. 3:18.

modern man, and he feels not only justified, but progressive. Like every other serious matter, to be at home with God, so that one associates with Him gladly and feels the joy of His presence, requires practice. It must be willed and carried out with much self-conquest, again and again. Then God gives us as a grace the sense of His holy presence.

So we shall have to learn that asceticism is an element of every life that is rightly lived. We shall do well if we practice setting limits to our urges, for the sake of proper measure. We shall learn to leave that which is less important but very attractive in order to attend to that which is more important. We shall take ourselves in hand in order to be spiritually free.

For example (we trust the reader will not mistake accuracy for pedantry), before going into the city we might resolve not to let ourselves be caught by advertisements and by people, but to keep our mind occupied with a fine thought or recollected in quiet freedom. Or we might turn off the radio so that the room will be still. Perhaps we might remain at home one evening instead of going out, or say no sometimes when eating or drinking or smoking — or many things of that sort. As soon as we turn our attention to the matter, we shall find many occasions for a liberating practice: learning to endure pain instead of resorting immediately to medication; accepting inwardly the renunciation that may be salutary for us; greeting an uncongenial person with quiet friendliness.

These and other such actions are not great things. We are not speaking of strict fasting or night vigils or difficult penances, but of practice in right living; of the truth that our life is different from that of the animal. It is human life, in which the internal drives are lifted by the spirit into a glorious but dangerous freedom. This spirit gives them their motive force, but it must also supply the regulating power, by means of which life is not destroyed, but brought to its fullness.

Courage

This meditation shall deal with courage — or bravery. The two words have related meanings, but there are slight differences. *Bravery* refers to behavior in concrete situations; *courage* refers to the general attitude, the manner in which one meets life. The terms shall be used as seems most suitable in each case.

First of all, we shall consider the distinction which we have found useful on several other occasions; that is, the distinction between a natural disposition and a moral attitude.

There is a kind of courage that is a natural quality. It may be that the person in question has no great sensitivity, and matters that would trouble another do not even enter his consciousness. His imagination is not very active, and he does not envision possible perils. So he passes through dangerous situations interiorly untouched or handles them easily. This is an excellent predisposition for practical living, but the one so predisposed must guard against becoming careless or brutal.

It can also happen that courage comes from a sound and healthy constitution, a strong *joie de vivre* which regards difficulties and dangers as a challenge; a confidence in life, secure in the feeling that things will turn out for the best. This is fine and may be what we would call "a good stock." Of course this, too, has its dangers, and the person so disposed must take care that he remains thoughtful — and thankful.

Finally there is a predisposition to courage which belongs to the realm of the noble and unusual. For one so disposed, bravery and honor are the same thing. He is aware of the challenge of life and feels bound by self-respect to meet it. He may not be very strong physically, and is perhaps very sensitive to suffering and therefore particularly subject to distress both exterior and interior. Nevertheless he stands firm, goes on quietly, and meets events without fear. This is a natural nobility which may also foredoom such a person to a tragic destiny.

All this is a matter of natural disposition. One has it or does not have it, and it may result in either good or evil. If a person so endowed comes under the influence of good teachers and recognizes his own possibilities, then a useful, good, and even noble life may result. But here we are speaking of something which — except in very unfavorable circumstances — is possible for everyone and hence may be a moral obligation, something which can be demanded of us, and for which we should train ourselves.

What would be the aspects of such a virtue? How would it develop and reveal itself? Let us begin with the main point which determines everything else, and which is the most difficult to realize. I mean the courage to accept one's own existence. We have spoken of this in our earlier reflections. Our existence is a tissue of good and bad, joyful and sorrowful, of things that assist and support us and also of those that hinder and burden us. Courage means the ability not only to select what pleases us or makes life easy, but also to accept the whole as it is, in the confidence that it reveals the Providence of God.

Every man bears within himself that mysterious something which we call his essential character. It means that qualities are not just jumbled together, but form a whole, something integrated and decisive which supports us but also makes demands. Each element aids the others but also brings with it a danger and burden for the others. This essential character man brings with him into life. It determines what he is and what he can accomplish, favorable and unfavorable — "himself." Courage means that he accepts this basic form of his existence in its entirety, not choosing or rejecting anything.

For example, one cannot be a person of strong sensibilities and choose to feel joy but not pain, for the one implies the other. To be sensitive is a glorious thing. It bestows great things upon us: the beauties of the world, the depths of personal relations, the tensions of struggle, and the joy of accomplishment. But this same sensitivity brings evil with it: the pain of loss, the sorrows of human conflict, and the fruitlessness of labor. We cannot have the one without the other.

So courage means, first of all, accepting oneself as one is, with the sensitivity of feeling and the painful experiences that it brings, as well as the precious gifts that it bestows. This does not mean that we must approve of everything — certainly not. But first we must accept, and then try to see what we can change, increase, moderate, or improve.

The integrated whole of which we have spoken means something else. It is like a picture which stands before us and which we can survey, but it is also like a melody which goes on in time, a configuration which is experienced as it transpires. The basic principle is the same, for what happens to a person is not just a matter of choice but corresponds to what he is. Character and destiny are intimately related.

The person who is not technically and economically minded will not experience what the person so minded will experience when he establishes a business, knows the triumph of success and the pain of failure. These things are granted to the one and denied to the other. But in return, the other person may have a natural appreciation of art and discover in it realities which the other never attains. A third person may be a scholar, perhaps a historian. He lives in all ages, understands the greatness of their achievements, and feels the grief of their passing away — all of which remains unknown to the other two.

To the differences of temperament and character we must add those of sex, of health, of social conditions, and so forth, all of which help to determine that in a certain life, some things take place and others do not.

So the existence of every man contains a pattern, a configuration of being and of events, and he must accept it as it is, and not desire to have the good without the bad. But he must first accept and affirm the whole, and then, certainly, do what he can to give it the form that he considers right and proper.

But in order to solve the problem, which is so vitally the problem of mankind, we must delve more deeply.

We may attempt to express the nature of man in various ways. In connection with the subject which we are discussing, we can do so by saying that man has a relation to the world as a whole. The animal is enclosed in its environment, and even though this environment may be enlarged in the process of evolution of the individual and the species, it remains essentially a partial thing. Only man is related to the whole world; he is himself a microcosm.

Of course he, too, is individually limited and hemmed in by all the qualifications of nationality and country, talents, sex, culture, social position, vocation or employment, and so forth; that is, by the very character of which we have spoken. But this contains a basic relation to the world as a whole, that which has been called the "microcosmic" element in man. This blending of individuality and universality composes the peculiarity of man: he is limited and at the same time related to the universe.

This tension in the character of man is bound up with another: the tension between necessity and freedom. Man lives under the universal laws, but bears within himself an abyss from which he can always draw a new beginning.

So, if he wishes to be true to reality, he must accept his limitations and his determination by the form of his character, but, because of his freedom in relation to the world, he has the ability of advancing toward the whole in his special way.

All this comes from God. He has given me to myself. I must accept my existence from His hand, must live it and carry it out. That is the basic courage, and how necessary it is today when there is so much talk of nothingness, destruction, oppressive fear, disgust, and dark things of all kinds. In large part, this is merely talk, and those who speak and write in this way, do not take it seriously themselves. But it is true that our time is really hard-pressed, from without and from within. It is a time of transition, in which a great deal is crumbling away, often without our being able to see what new structure shall take its place. Therefore it is doubly necessary that we confidently accept our existence from God and live it courageously.

This interior form of the individual being and life involves a practice of courage which a person of strong and cheerful temperament may not be consciously aware of, but which some may feel as a difficult task: the confidence requisite for living with a view to the future, for acting, building, assuming responsibilities, and forming ties. For, in spite of our precautions, the future is, in each case, the unknown. But living means advancing into this unknown region, which may lie before us like a chaos into which we must venture.

Here everyone must make the venture in the confidence that the future is not a chaos or a totally strange thing. Rather, his own character, the ordering power within him, will make a way so that it is really his own future into which he moves.

This also forms the natural basis for the message of Christ about the Providence which guards every man — the message that the future, although all unknown, is not strange, not hostile, but is arranged for him by God; that existence, although it extends far beyond our ken, is not a chaos, but ordered by God for him.

To believe this and live accordingly may be difficult for a person who is of a hesitant or timid disposition. But here the courage to live coincides with trust in the divine guidance.

There is another point that we must consider, something particularly pressing in times when historical epochs end and new ones begin. This is man's relation to the future as a whole, to the course of history. The life of the individual does not flow along in the course of history like water in the bed of a stream;

rather it forms a part of it. Sometimes the individual is so bound up with the past that the future is quite strange to him. Then he lives without confidence in the future and takes refuge in the past. What has been is so completely satisfactory to him and its form so fair, that all that is new repels him.

Here, too, courage is necessary — courage which dares to face the future in the confidence that God's plan will work out. This courage accepts what is to come, sees in it the individual's own task, and cooperates. This may be very difficult and can be accomplished only by means of true obedience to the will of Him who guides history.

Bravery means standing one's ground in danger. What is the root of all that we call danger? It is the evil which affects all hearts and makes it possible for hostile elements to touch us. It is the hypersensitivity of our nature which can be offended in so many ways. It is mutability, which causes our life to move toward death. These are facts that cannot be changed. And bravery means facing these conditions of our existence and standing firm before them — indeed, standing firm before life as it comes, first of all, because one overcomes danger more easily if one goes to meet it than if one is intimidated by it; also, because one surmounts pain more easily if one bears it freely than if one becomes wrapped up in it. Moreover, difficulties are a part of our life. They are sent to us. If we meet them bravely, they prove to be a gain. Every situation contains a possibility for growth, for becoming a better man — the man we were meant to be. We waste this opportunity if we seek to evade the difficulty.

The courage that accepts life and meets it bravely in each instance implies a conviction that there is something within us that cannot be destroyed, but rather which derives nourishment from everything, becomes stronger, richer, and deeper through every experience rightly faced and carried out, because this something comes from the creative power of God.

Actually, this something is the power of God itself. If, in a favorable hour, I penetrate quietly and recollectedly into the inmost depths of my being, ever more deeply until I reach, as it were, the interior boundary of nothingness — there I find God's power which maintains me in existence. This preserving power is indestructible, even though I pass through danger and through death. The reason for all present-day talk of anxiety and dissolution and nothingness, for all the grotesque figures of art and poetry, and for the overwhelming force of political power is that the consciousness of interior support, the confidence in the hand of God in the depths, at the edge of nothingness, is no longer alive in men.

There is another kind of courage of which we must speak; that is, the courage to take a risk if it is God's will. To everyone there comes in some way the call of God, and it decides his life. This call may take various forms. It may be a question of the occupation a man is to choose. So much depends on whether he chooses the lifework of which his deepest self says, "This is where you belong; to this you are 'called,' " or whether he chooses something that promises more money, easier success, or greater human respect!

It may also be a question of a person, a friend, or a love. Again what matters is whether man permits himself to be drawn into something that is alluring, flatters his self-esteem, yet of which his deepest self warns him that it may deprive him of what is highest; or, whether he chooses that which may be harder, more demanding, but which builds life and teaches responsibility.

There are also lesser decisions. Basically, every admonition of conscience is a call of God. For the good is not simply the useful or that which conduces to a fuller life or the progress of a culture; it is the holiness of God which urges man to admit it into his life, and which is embodied in the ethical demands of each situation. Each situation is a call, for it addresses us and says, "Do this — do not do that!" Again and again, we are faced with the decision: to dare to tell the truth or to lie, to be just or to seek our own advantage, to be pure or to permit ourselves to be defiled, to be noble or to slip into the mean and low. On each occasion, God calls us.

Here courage means placing our hand in His and following Him, in small things and in great. The way may lead us very far. We know of persons who follow it so far that they escape our comprehension; these are the saints. We hear them speak, we read their writings, but essentially they have gone beyond us, with God. This is the highest challenge.

If there is a regret which is most bitter at life's end, it is this: I heard the call but did not follow it.

In our reflections, we have always applied the virtue we were considering to God and attempted to know Him better in the light of that virtue. Can we also speak of courage in connection with God? We can, if we remove from it all that is merely human and which, if applied to God, would detract from His holy sovereignty.

When was God, in this highest sense, courageous? He was courageous when He created man, when He "decided" — using the word with all the reservations we must apply to every statement which brings God in relation to time — to create beings who possess freedom, and to put His world into their hands. But this meant — speaking once more with the proper reservations — that He put His honor in their hands. For God created the world in wisdom and in love. He called it "good" and "very good,"[35] and it is so forever. These creatures — mankind — could be faithful, but they could also revolt against Him. And yet he dared to expose His work to the danger of their freedom.

And when the danger became a reality and man refused to obey Him, God took a second "risk," so inconceivably great that it requires the whole power of confident faith not to be scandalized by it. He Himself took on the responsibility for man's guilt. He became man, and accepted a destiny in our confused history.

Have we ever thought about the truly divine courage of Christ? Have we understood the bravery that fired the heart of Jesus, when He, who came from the presence — St. John says "from the bosom"[36] — of the Father, stepped into this earthly world, into all the falsehood, the murderous cruelty, and the pitiful narrowness of our existence? And He did this, not protected by the pride of the philosopher or secured by the tactics of the politician, not willing to repay guile with guile and blow with blow, but in the vulnerability of perfect purity.

Let us consider how we act amid the dangers of this world; how energetically we protect ourselves by all manner of means. Jesus never protected Himself, but He accepted everything

[35]Gen. 1:10, 31.
[36]John 1:18.

that the violence and unscrupulousness of men inflicted upon Him. We do not take the world as it is, but choose from it what pleases us. He accepted what the course of events brought upon Him, for this was the will of the Father. We know how to conform, to evade, and to seek advantages. His nature was such, and He spoke and acted in such a manner that what was most evil in men was challenged; in such a manner that, as we read in Luke's Gospel, "the thoughts," the hidden disposition, "in the hearts of many were revealed."[37]

He truly lived in the conditions of the world and endured them. The hour of Gethsemane lets us surmise what that meant. If we try to fathom all this, we may well shudder before what we can call the courage of God in Christ.

And He dared to live this life not in order to accomplish something of earthly grandeur, glorious heroism, or a noble work of art, but as a redemption, for our sake. He lived so that we might gain the courage to be Christians in the world in which He was Christ.

To the extent to which we put away illusions and see how much so-called Christian morality and Christian culture is actually the product of a particular historical situation; to the extent to which we experience how the world does all the things which St. John in the prologue of his Gospel tells us of its behavior toward the incarnate Son of God; only to that extent shall we realize that the attempt to be Christians in this world and to order our existence in accord with Christ appears to be a most desperate undertaking. Then it becomes clear what, in the final analysis, is meant by *courage*, that is, the

[37]Luke 2:35.

attitude which says, "But nevertheless," and takes up the battle in spite of all that makes it appear senseless and vain. We must never forget that He has fought the fight before us and thereby made it possible for us to conquer.

Kindness

In this chapter, we shall speak of a virtue which is easily neglected because it is reserved, inconspicuous, and quiet; that is, the virtue of kindness. How often we speak of love! It challenges us, for it is noble and radiant. But we should speak of it less often — that would be better for it — and instead should speak of that which our callous age needs so sorely: kindness.

This word often misleads us to regard what it designates in a derogatory fashion, to misunderstand *kindness* as mere good nature, which is certainly nothing very valuable. Good nature is passivity, which lets things take their course; or indolence, which avoids conflict; or even stupidity, which believes anything. But kindness is something deep and strong, and for that reason, it is not easy to define.

Let us attempt it in this way: a kind person is one who is well disposed toward life. But can one be ill disposed toward life? Yes, indeed, especially if we are dealing not so much with overt actions as with the disposition behind them, which may perhaps escape our notice.

It may be that a person desires to dominate others. He says that he desires their best interests, but actually what he wishes is to dominate. Such a person is not well disposed toward life, for life is smothered in the grasp of tyranny. Many a domestic tragedy results from the fact that one person wishes to dominate others. It may be the husband or the wife, a son or a daughter. True kindness allows to life a proper space and freedom of movement; it even gives and provides these, for only in this way can life grow and develop.

Or it may be that a person is resentful toward life. He thinks that he has suffered an injustice; his expectations have been disappointed; his claims have been disregarded. This may perhaps really be the case, and he should try to make the best of the possibilities that remain. But he cannot overcome the feeling of resentment, and he takes revenge. "They are all like that," he says, because one was like that. "There is no justice," he says, because he thinks he has not been given justice. Kindness pardons, for it is magnanimous and releases the offender; it trusts and always allows life to begin anew.

Much unkindness results from envy. Many a poor person sees another man enjoying his wealth. In some way or another, everyone feels that others have what he lacks. If he cannot accept this fact, becomes bitter, and envies the other his possessions, then his mind is poisoned and he becomes an enemy of life. Kindness can look beyond itself; it does not begrudge to others what it lacks. In fact, it can even rejoice with the others. We might mention many similar things.

Kindness means that a person is well disposed toward life. Whenever he encounters a living being, the kind man's first reaction is not to mistrust and criticize but to respect, to value, and to promote development. Life is sorely in need of this attitude — our human life — which is so vulnerable.

But in kindness there is strength — strength in proportion to its purity — and perfect kindness is inexhaustible. Life is full of suffering; if a person is well disposed toward life, then suffering touches him and makes itself felt. But that is wearing. Suffering demands our understanding; and that requires exertion. It demands help. But only he who truly understands the suffering in any particular case can really help; only he who can find the necessary words and can see what must be done in order to alleviate the suffering. Woe unto that kindness if it is merely well disposed but is weak. It can happen that it is destroyed by its own sympathy or, in order to protect itself, becomes violent.

True kindness requires patience. Suffering returns again and again and demands understanding. The failings of others touch us repeatedly and become the more unendurable because we know them by heart. Kindness must constantly make the effort and turn to the others.

One other thing is required by kindness, something of which we rarely speak: a sense of humor. It helps us to endure things more easily. Indeed we could hardly get along without it. The person who sees man only seriously, only morally or pedagogically, cannot endure him for any great length of time. We must have an eye for the oddity of existence. Everything human has something comic about it. The more pompously a man acts, the greater is the comic element. A sense of humor means that we take man seriously and strive to help him, but suddenly see how odd he is, and laugh, even though it be only inwardly. A friendly laugh at the oddity of all human affairs — that is humor. It helps us to be kind, for after a good laugh, it is easier to be serious again.

Learning the Virtues

One thing more must be said about kindness: it is quiet. True kindness does not talk much, does not seek attention, does not fuss with organizations and statistics, does not photograph and analyze. The deeper it goes, the more silent it grows. It is the daily bread by which life is nourished. When this disappears, there may be science and politics and welfare, but in the end, all remains cold.

And now we shall seek for kindness in the place from which all virtue comes; we shall seek for it in God.

God is essentially good. In the Psalms, the prayerbook of the Old Testament, we find beautiful statements about God's goodness. And they are authentic, for the men of the Old Testament were not soft-hearted; they could not be so, in view of the hard life they were compelled to live. Israel was a small nation and lived in a poor land; indeed, half of it was a stony desert. The Israelites were always in danger, for around them lurked powerful cultures, wealthy and filled with the pride and luxury of paganism, hostile to the pure faith of divine revelation. When an Israelite spoke of the goodness and kindness of God, it was the result of a genuine experience. So we read, for example, in the 144th Psalm: "The Lord is gracious and merciful, patient and plenteous in mercy. The Lord is sweet to all, and His tender mercies are over all His works."[38]

If we could see God's goodness, this abyss of kindness, we would be joyful all our life long. That a world exists at all is a continuous expression of God's goodness. The world would not exist if He did not wish it. He does not need it for Himself. How could the infinite God need the world, which disappears

[38]Ps. 144:8-9 (RSV = Ps. 145:8-9).

before Him? If He creates it and preserves it, it is because of His goodness and kindness.

But now someone will ask, "Does the world look as if God were well disposed toward it? Does human existence appear to be a work of divine goodness?" Anyone who is honest will answer, "Certainly not." Again and again, man questions God: "Why all this if You are good?" The question is not unreasonable if it arises from an afflicted heart. But in itself it is foolish, for what is the source of all the evil that embitters man's existence? Man himself is responsible.

When the complaint arises that God cannot be good, or even that there cannot be a God when everything is as it is, the person who speaks in this way rarely asks or thinks what the reason for all the evil may be. But the fact is that God put His world in man's hands so that man in cooperation with his Creator might construct that existence which the book of Genesis shows us under the figure of Paradise. But man was not willing. He wished to construct not God's kingdom but his own. This brought all that is confused, false, and destructive into the action of man. How, then, can he rise up and say, "If You, God, were good, You would not have created such a world"? And the disorder which man brings into existence continues and is increased even by the very person who utters the complaint.

And it is a fact that each one of us makes life a bit worse. Every evil or unkind word that we utter poisons the atmosphere. Every falsehood, every act of violence enters into existence and increases its confusion. We ourselves have made life what it is. So it is dishonest if we say that God cannot be good when everything is as it is. We can only say, "Lord, give me patience to endure what we have brought about. Help me to do what I can to make things better where I am." That is the only honest reply.

But we might raise another objection and ask how God can be good when the world of the animals, those beings which cannot be bad, includes so much pain. Many a melancholy person has not been able to handle that problem. How can God's goodness watch over the world when innocent creatures constantly endure so much terrible suffering? I will be honest: I know no answer.

But one thought has helped me, and perhaps it will help others. Let us consider what *goodness* means if the term is predicated of God. We have the right — and the duty — to form concepts from the reflection of God's being upon objects and upon our own life, concepts by which we attempt to grasp what He is. So we can say that God is just, God has patience, God is kind, and so forth — all the important statements in which we transfer the magnitude and beauty of creation, freed from imperfection, to Him who created all.

But if we look closely, what, for example, does the statement "God is just" mean? We know what the word *just* means when it is applied to man, for we are finite beings and can be comprehended by finite concepts. But what if we apply the word to God, who is beyond all measures and concepts? Do we still comprehend the meaning of the word *just*? Is it not, so to speak, taken out of our hands?

Our thinking and speaking of God must proceed in this way: all finite beings receive their nature from Him. So we take one characteristic of these beings, put it into words, apply it to God, and say, "He is like that, only in an absolutely perfect manner as the prototype of the finite copy." But thereby the word is, in a sense, swallowed up by the divine abyss, and we can only revere His infinitude. This is the case here. If, for instance, I say of a mother that she is kind and her whole family lives by her kindness, then I know what the sentence means, and no truth more beautiful can be expressed. But what if I say God is kind? At first I seem to know what I mean, but then the mystery seizes upon the word and removes it from my grasp. Yet a direction of meaning remains, like the shining trail left by a meteor when it disappears in immeasurable space. A stillness remains, which perceives the direction, an awe which trembles before the mystery and becomes adoration.

For our problem, this means that God is kind and good even then, when we do not understand His goodness.

Understanding

Human society is not an apparatus whose parts are fitted into each other so that they form a smoothly running whole. Rather, it consists of individuals, each of whom, in spite of all similarity of place and time, has his own particular character. Each has his own development, his purposes, and his destiny. Each one forms a living entity rooted in itself. Of course, individuals are bound together by various relations: by birth, education, friendship, dependency in their profession or work, and so forth. But every person has his own center which relates experiences and activities to itself and so stands apart from the general context. Moreover, in each individual, there are forces hostile to other living beings, which make association difficult and may even destroy it.

What is necessary in order that an association may become not merely possible, but fruitful? We might name many things. One is understanding. And that is no small matter.

What does it mean? When do I understand? When I notice what the other person, with whom I am dealing, means. When I see why he acts as he does, why he lives as he does, and why he has become the person who now faces me.

Learning the Virtues

In order to see more clearly what is involved, we shall look at other creatures who also live in a society, that is, the animals. Do they understand each other? They are bound together by various relations and are dependent on each other in many ways. Let us, for example, consider the birds. They pair off at a definite time, feed and protect their young, and help them to become independent. Do they understand each other? We might think that they do, for each one behaves in the way that is best for the other and for the young. They help each other to live; therefore, we think they must understand each other.

But this is far from being the case. A simple fact proves this: as soon as the young are grown, they become strangers to each other. Here there is no understanding involved, but the two beings who are mated, and then the pair and the young who spring forth from their life, form a cycle of life, a whole, whose preservation is guaranteed by instincts which otherwise work only for the individual and which disappear when the biological purpose has been fulfilled. It is just because they do not "understand" each other, just because in their relations there is no doubt or time of testing, that the whole process takes place with such expediency and security.

Or let us think of creatures that live in an enduring association and for whose conduct we like to employ sociological concepts, such as ants or bees. Their associations consist of numerous individuals, each of whom performs one function within the whole. They pass each other without disturbing each other; even more, they help and defend each other, and they build up a complicated living structure with marvelous cooperation. Do they understand each other? We call their association a "state," but is it really that? This would assume that within it, at least in certain situations, there takes place a conscious self-subordination of the individual and hence a mutual understanding. But this is not the case, and the whole image of a "state" is basically false.

If we wish to express the situation correctly, we should rather think of the relation that exists between the cells of an organism. An anthill is like a single living being, whose cell-animals are not regulated by a mutual understanding but by an instinctively operating general plan, although this expression does not really explain very much.

Where, then, can we speak of an understanding? Where the situation involves beings in each of whom there is an inner life which is hidden and yet expressed in the exterior activity and so can be perceived by another being of the same kind.

Someone approaches me on the street, looks at me, and tips his hat. From this action, I can see that his attention is directed toward me, that he "means" me. By the expression on his face I can tell whether the man with whom I am dealing is well disposed toward me or has an aversion to me or feels embarrassed.

Someone explains his behavior to me on a certain occasion, which had surprised me. I hear his words; their meaning becomes clear to me. Now I know what I could not know before.

These and countless other incidents, which constantly occur, indicate that man carries an interior world within himself; that dispositions, conditions, and feelings, which are originally hidden, can be expressed in words, countenance, attitude, behavior, and actions, and so can be revealed.

Understanding, then, means being able to read or grasp the interior meaning in consequence of the external manifestation. But the external can also conceal the interior meaning. If a person is troubled but does not wish to show it, he "controls himself," checks the play of expression, and assumes a quiet mien. The interior processes, conditions, and emotions then lie behind the visible manifestation, or beneath or within it, by whatever term we wish to express the relation, depending on the particular viewpoint of our consideration.

What would understanding mean then? We might use the word if the other person were so sensitive that he could tell by the expression of the eyes or some slight movements not wholly controlled, or by details of bodily posture, what is really going on — and also that it is concealed. Understanding could go even farther. We might notice that the other person does not merely hide his feelings but shows something which he does not feel at all; that he wishes to deceive, is hypocritical in his gestures of friendship, or pretends interest when he is really indifferent. Then understanding would mean seeing through this whole pretense, noting what the truth really is, and also noting the other person's dishonesty.

Therefore, we see that understanding is a thing of many strata. Here understanding means to see, to hear, and to perceive how, behind a feeling that is manifested, behind an opinion that is expressed, something else is hidden — and perhaps another thing behind that.

But true understanding goes even farther. If someone becomes gruff and surly at a particular moment, then understanding means seeing how this feeling fits into the whole of his nature. A certain way of acting expresses different things on the part of different persons. When a shy person becomes gruff because he wishes to hide his inmost feelings, it is something quite different than when an impudent person becomes violent in order to get his way. He who truly understands also sees the whole context in which a gesture or movement or word acquires its full meaning.

And this holds true not only of the context of disposition and temperament, but also of time. Why is one person so timid? Because in the past, he suffered violence. Why is he distrustful? Because he has often been deceived. What causes the curious look of sadness and of expectation in his eyes? He has found little understanding in his life and yearns for it. So understanding also means recognizing how the present hour results from a man's life history.

All this is not easy — and yet we have been dealing only with simple things. What if we are dealing with unusual dispositions, morbid conditions, and particular destinies, in the face of which the powers of seeing, hearing, and feeling must become positively creative in order to comprehend and penetrate the rare phenomenon?

What, then, is demanded so that we may truly learn to understand?

Many things are necessary. First, there is a talent for this — a keenness of sight, a delicacy of feeling, an ability to put oneself in another's place — which bridges the distance between persons. These are important qualities which establish community between many individuals. They may be highly developed and make the one who possesses them either an artist, a leader, a sage — or else a person who exploits the weaknesses of others and maliciously despises them.

Experience is necessary. This means not merely that something has happened to me in the past, happened perhaps many times, but also that I am capable of learning from it, that I gain from my various experiences a clearer view, a finer perception, and a quicker sympathy. *Experience* means also that in the face of other persons' behavior, we remember things perceived in the past which are similar to those which are taking place and which, as it were, provide a key to their meaning.

What else is proper to understanding? Let us approach the matter from another angle. Why is understanding so rare? Why do so many persons meet again and again and yet not understand each other? For this is certainly the case; otherwise they would act differently, and the atmosphere around them would be clearer.

There are many reasons for this. Let us consider just one. We tend to classify people at once into those whom we like and those whom we do not like. Consequently, people are divided by our self-love into two great compartments and labeled accordingly. This is done so instinctively that a whole sociology has been built upon the relation of amity and enmity.

Understanding is essentially human and begins only when we step out of this relation of congeniality or antipathy and try to accept the other person as he is; it begins when we do not classify him at once according to our likes and dislikes, our purposes and apprehensions, but say, "You have a right to exist; be as you are. You are yourself just as I am myself." Then our view becomes clear, and understanding can come about.

For example, what about a friendship? It can prosper only when one does not judge the other according to the purpose for which he can use him, but permits him simply to be who he is; when the relation of amity and enmity, in the sense in which we have spoken of it, does not come into consideration, but two persons stand face to face in freedom and respect. Only then can we see clearly and understand.

Or what about a marriage? If one party demands of the other that he should be as he would have him, then the two may be married for thirty years and yet not understand each other; indeed, what is worse, they may misunderstand each other with a stubborn obstinacy which is incomprehensible to a third person, and each of the two reproaches the other with doing what he himself does.

The beginning of all understanding consists in this: that each one shall give the other freedom to be what he is, and not regard him from the point of view of egotism, prescribing for him what he is to be according to one's own self-interest, but rather regarding him from the point of view of freedom, first saying, "Be what you are," and then, "Now I should like to know what you are, and why."

This is the attitude that brings about understanding. It presupposes that we give the other person the right to be himself; that we do not regard him as a piece of our own environment which we can use, but as a being who has his own original center, his way of life, and his own wishes and rights. Only then can we rightly ask, "Why does he do that? What experiences has he had? What is the history behind his behavior? How are his various attitudes related to each other? Is the gruffness which he shows really violence or only a kind of shame which hides what is within? Is his impatience really such or only the hurt resulting from previous experiences?"

And so on. Only then will the questions really find an answer, the answer of understanding.

All this is so indispensable that we may venture to state the paradox that we learn really to understand ourself only when we regard ourself from another's point of view. Would not a physician gain an entirely new insight into his own behavior if he suddenly asked himself, "How do my patients see me?" Not, "How would I like them to see me," but, "How do they really see me, from their own point of view?" Not the admirers but the ordinary ones, the poor, those who suffer greatly. Then he would gain a very sober view of himself, and this would be very useful to him as a physician.

Or suppose a teacher asked himself, "How do my students see me?" Those students are by no means the stupid, rebellious creatures he often considers them, but they frequently have very sharp eyes and good judgment. He would have to ask himself in very concrete fashion, "How do they see me when I enter the room, when I call on them, when one has done poor work or when there is a disturbance?" Perhaps he would suddenly understand the opposition to him.

In a marriage, the husband might ask himself, "How does my wife see me on this occasion or on another?" And conversely the wife might ask, "How does my husband see me?" Not, "How would I like him to see me?" but, "How does he really see me? How do my attitude, my voice, and my demands affect him?" Then each one might suddenly see very clearly whether his love is genuine, when dishonesty creeps in or brutality shows itself.

To do this is not easy. We must often attempt it and must practice this viewing of ourselves from the other person's viewpoint. If we are successful in seeing ourselves without the egotism that distorts the picture, then what we see may be very unpleasant, but it will help us to get at the truth.

This also helps us to do something else: to judge others better; and this is necessary in order to live rightly.

The word *judge* here does not mean that against which Jesus warns us when he says, "Judge not." He who does this, usurps the right to say, "This person can stay as he is; that one must change. This one has the right to be; the other must be removed," and so on. To such persons Jesus says, "Judge not, that you may not be judged."[39] But we mean that evaluation of another which helps us to do justice to his value, to see his defects as they are, in order to establish the right relationship with him, in confidence and in caution. Most judgments of people about each other basically mean only, "I find this person pleasant, that one unpleasant; this person I can use, the other not." A true judgment would say, "This person is suited to the task at hand; that one would mismanage the matter," and so on. But all this is possible only if we have first understood the other person's true nature.

Every genuine virtue extends from earth to Heaven, or, more correctly, from Heaven to earth. Does God "understand"? Indeed He does, and this understanding transcends all human measures.

God knows every being from its inmost core. This is so not because He gazes so deeply into it and tests it so exactly, but because He has thought it and brought it into existence. Let us think of God's creative power in the right way. His creating

[39]Matt. 7:1.

does not mean making — fitting something to particular purposes — but, with effortless power, calling a creature into existence and setting it free. God's creating is so perfect and magnanimously liberal that He not only brought man into real being, but placed him in a condition of true freedom.

It has often been asked how man can be free if God is omnipotent, whether His boundless might would not overpower the puny freedom of man as the stream overpowers the drifting leaf. The answer is this: My friend, how insufficient is your concept of God's omnipotence! His power is one with His magnanimity and His reverence; it is this that sets you free. Only in God's eye and hand do you become master of yourself. And if you say that is a paradox — no, the marvel is that if there is an Infinite One, finite beings can also exist. But it is presumption if you with your puny intellect claim that you can grasp it.

At this point, we might look back. The joy that God takes in every man, the magnanimity with which he sets him free, and the pure understanding which is not subsequent to the being of things, but establishes it, should teach us, for God has granted us the privilege of being His image.

What would be the purest fulfillment of the meaning of friendship? If friends could feel this about each other: "In his glance I am wholly myself. His glance does not hem me in, does not reproach me with what I am, but in its light, I become entirely myself."

It would be a perfect marriage in which the wife could feel that in the eyes of her husband, she reached completeness of being, and conversely the husband found his purest and truest self in the understanding of his wife — if each could see himself in the eyes of the other as that which he was meant to be. Not that vanity imagines a consort such as could not exist, but that love sees the possibilities which are still dormant in the other.

Courtesy

In the twelfth chapter of his letter to the Romans, St. Paul writes about the communion of the redeemed and says great things about it. He speaks of the mysterious powers which dwelt in the communities of the early period, and says, "Be fervent in spirit" — a sentence which should remind us to what great things we are called, and how puny and feeble our response really is. In the midst of these lofty words, we find the simple statement, "Anticipate one another in showing honor";[40] not merely, "Honor one another," but, "Anticipate one another in showing honor." Perhaps we might translate the sentence in everyday language as, "Be courteous to each other."

Now, we might ask how St. Paul, who had such noble things to say, could bother about anything like that. But he knew that in our life, everything fits together, the extraordinary and the commonplace, the fervor of spirit and the manner of behavior that grows out of reverence for other men. For example, St. Paul himself, who proclaimed the mystery of the

[40]Rom. 12:10.

mystical body of Christ,[41] also wrote to the congregation in Philippi that Evodias and Syntyche should stop quarreling.[42] These were two women who were active in the service of the community, but, as happens today also, evidently couldn't get along with each other. Various similar things can be found in the apostle's letters. If he found time, amid his great concerns, to talk about such everyday matters, we can do the same.

In these meditations, we have spoken of noble virtues: justice, truthfulness, selflessness, and many others. But courtesy also is a virtue and worth considering.

If I may be permitted, I would like to recount a personal recollection: a long time ago, when I was still attending school, a woman whom I greatly revered said to me one day, "Do not forget that there is a great love of our neighbor, but also a small one! The great one has its occasion when there is a great need to be met or when it becomes dangerous to remain loyal. But there is always an occasion for the small one, because it belongs to our everyday life. It is courtesy." I have never forgotten these words.

What, then, is courtesy?

Originally, as we can easily see, the word *courtesy* denoted proper behavior at the court of the ruler, in a noble environment. Then it lost this particular meaning and took on a more general one: proper behavior as such, the result of a good upbringing; it is in this sense that we shall use it.

People live together in narrow spaces: within a house, an office, a factory, in conference rooms, in the crowded streets,

[41]Cf. 1 Cor. 12:27.
[42]Phil. 4:2.

in traffic, and in the limited confines of a densely populated country. Consequently their spheres of action are always touching each other. Their purposes cross just as their paths do. Here there is constant danger of friction, of the kindling of anger; and every sensible person wishes to encounter courtesy. He will try to find forms which express concern for a proper association of the multitudes, which lessen the violence of antagonism and of cross-purposes, and which move people to be obliging and enable them to receive consideration from others.

This is courtesy. It is an everyday affair, but how important for the whole of life!

Now, one might think that this would happen spontaneously. It would — if man were an animal. Everybody has probably, at one time or another, stood before an anthill and watched the swarming, teeming activity. Each one of the tiny creatures found its way and did not interfere with the others. Each one performed its task without hindrance. Sometimes a burden became too heavy; then a second ant took hold and helped. And if the observer perhaps gave way to the childish temptation and disturbed the little community, then all ran about in great turmoil at first, but then each one set to work and soon everything was in order again.

We might think that if animals can do this, man should certainly be better able to do it. But it is quite the other way. Just because he is man, he cannot do it so simply and easily; for the animals live by instinct, which is an expression of organic necessity. But in man, mind is operative, and "mind" means that man can recognize truth, but can also err. The animal does not err in matters concerned with the conduct of its life. If it does, it is sick and it perishes. But man can err and is confronted with the task of learning. Man can make mistakes. If an animal does this, it is because an obstacle was in the way, either exterior or interior; but man can act wrongly because his judgment may be incorrect or passion may mislead him.

Therefore he must be watchful and careful in his association with others, so that it does not become a struggle with every man's hand against every other man. This watchfulness is expressed in ethics and moral education, in law and in the administration of justice. These are the great things. But it is manifested also in the forms of everyday communication, in courtesy, and we must say at once that these little things mean much more than one might suppose. A large section of moral life is included in them, just as moral degeneration is quickly manifested in a lowering of the tone of everyday communication.

Wherein does courteous behavior consist? If we wish to answer this question and look at the facts, we find a great variety of forms. There are some which can be understood at once, but also some that are strange and unusual. Many are natural and appropriate; others are artificial, even foolish. Can we discover basic forms upon which the manifold varieties are built? Perhaps we can.

There is first of all the will to give others room. Culture does not begin with obtrusiveness and with grasping; it begins with taking one's hands away and stepping back. Courtesy gives the other person a free space and protects him from oppressive closeness; it gives him air. It recognizes the good in others and lets them feel that it is valued. It keeps silence about one's own qualities and keeps these in the background, lest they discourage others. Courtesy strives to keep unpleasant things at a distance or at least to bridge them. It tries to avoid embarrassing situations, to remove the sting from difficult and painful circumstances, and to lighten burdens. It induces young people to honor their elders, men to honor women, and the strong to defer to the weak. All these are motives which moderate the impulses of insolence and violence and make life easier for others.

These motives lead the person who wishes to associate with others in proper fashion to behave in such a way that the possibilities of tension, of clash, and of mutual injury or offense are avoided, so that no evil may result. For man's nature includes all these possibilities.

Naturalism states that the animal from which man has evolved is still present within him. By bitter experience and repeated effort it has been tamed, but it is always ready to break out. But this is too simple a concept. The reality is much worse. It is tragically serious. Within man there lives his primeval ancestor who once broke out and renounced obedience to God. There live in man all of the ancestors from time immemorial who disobeyed again and again. It is not only wildness that lives in man, but also wickedness. This must be met by the serious and difficult struggle of moral self-education.

And courtesy is its simplest form. It lightens the difficulty and assists morality; indeed, it can sometimes substitute for it. Quite frequently moral difficulties are avoided by what we call "good manners," and entanglements which could lead to evil consequences are resolved without much trouble.

Learning the Virtues

Courtesy is very important and very helpful in our life. It is not a great act, such as standing beside someone in great danger or freeing him from some pressing need or distress, but it is one of the little things which lighten the ever-perceptible difficulties of life. It is consideration for the mood of our neighbor, sympathy for his weariness, smoothing over a painful situation, and so forth. A constant attempt to make life easier and to obviate the many, and often strange, threats that endanger it — this is courtesy.

Here belongs also that facilitating of life which St. Paul means when he says, "Anticipate one another in showing honor." But why does he use the noble expression "showing honor"? Because man possesses what we call "dignity."

A *thing* does not have dignity; it only requires the treatment suitable to its nature — unless we mean that deep, even mysterious quality which belongs to it as an essential structure, and which we perceive so keenly in a noble object. But dignity in the true sense of the word is found only in the person. A thing can be bought and sold, given and received, used and destroyed. All this is proper, as long as we act according to the nature of the thing. But this cannot be done in the case of a person.

The fact that we feel this marks the beginning of culture, as we have said, and it indicates a great and ever-increasing threat that man today is forced more and more into the role of a thing. But man is a person, and this means that every man is unique. No man can be replaced. His achievements, his work, and his property may be replaced, but not the man himself. Every man is unique, in his relation to God and in God's relation to him.

This uniqueness demands a special attitude on our part: honor. This is shown in our daily communications, by the forms of courtesy proper to every situation, and we might reconsider what has been said above concerning the basic acts of courtesy, and how honor is shown in each of them.

Finally we might point out that courtesy is a thing of beauty and makes life beautiful. It is "form": an attitude, gesture, or action which does not merely serve a purpose, but also expresses a meaning which has value in itself, namely, the dignity of man. At their highest point, these gestures and actions become a drama which represents a lofty mode of being — for example, in the ceremonies of state or in the ritual of liturgical celebrations. Of course, there is also the danger inherent in every symbol; that is, that it may become artificial, unnatural, and hence untrue.

But it is a fact that today courtesy is disintegrating everywhere. This is not a criticism of our culture, but is meant to bring to our attention something that concerns us all. Our life, influenced by science and technology, is largely determined by material objects, and this means that our attention is directed to the demands of the material situation, the work we are engaged in, or the end to be attained; and so we are inclined to banish the superfluous, in form and action, and to proceed directly and without any detour toward the matter at hand. This is necessary wherever time has been wasted and materials and work-power have been squandered. It produces a clear, clean style of action and structure which, under favorable circumstances, can attain to an austere beauty.

But it is likely to produce an atmosphere in which objectivity becomes coarseness. And this regards all that we have recognized as the object of reverence — the person; his dignity, feelings, and emotions; all the deep and tender things that indicate "life" — as nonessentials, insofar as they cannot be considered as items in an account. And that sympathy for another person, that consideration for his circumstances and his mood in each particular situation — everything that is part of courtesy — is then regarded as superfluous. The effect is disastrous; existence is impoverished and coarsened.

We must emphasize another point, something that has a direct effect on people's dealings with each other; namely, the lack of time. Courtesy requires time. In order to exercise it, we must stop and wait; we must make a detour; and we must be considerate and defer our own affairs. But all this takes time, and in our age of forced deadlines, of precisely functioning machinery, of the high costs of construction, and of fierce competition, the loss of time is something useless, irrational, erroneous, and even wicked.

And so, of course, courtesy dies. Sometimes that may be an advantage: formalities are dispensed with; matters that are merely external, and hence unnatural and untrue, such as might easily be bound up with courtesy, disappear. But courtesy itself disappears, and in its place we have at best a terse correctness. It is true that this may lead to something fine — an honesty that rejects whatever is not genuine, an understanding between those who consider the requirements of a task, or a friendliness which requires no words of reassurance. But these require a genuineness of character and a fine upbringing which are not easy to find or to attain.

And so that which we call "life" suffers a loss. For life does not go on according to the laws of labor-saving and of the preservation of materials. These are technical standards. Life takes detours; it squanders, or rather, consumes time. Life wants to linger, to delay for the "extra" things. A life deprived of the "extras," of "waste," becomes a mere mechanical process.

So we must be careful that the exigencies of time do not destroy our life. A man who loses courtesy for the sake of material objects becomes poor. And we must be honest and not conceal the fact that much indolence, indifference, and violence may hide behind our boasted realism and objectivity and turn the much-praised honesty into a falsehood far more unpleasant than that courtesy which was accused of being artificial.

But we can carry this thought farther, and then it may help us to a new insight.

How did the old-fashioned courtesy — the courtesy which we who are more advanced in years once learned — really originate? It evolved in the course of history and with respect to persons of high degree or, ultimately, the king. The history of civilization, and especially the history of religion, reveals this.

The very origin of the word draws our attention. Courtesy was originally something belonging to the court. It was the kind of behavior demanded by the presence of the king. In the thoughts of the men of old, the king approached divinity, was himself something divine. Therefore, he was worthy of special reverence, as a revelation of the sublime, and reverence was also due to the rays of divinity which he shed over the whole of earthly existence. These rays continued downward; in various steps the sublime descended, so to speak, and on each level, it exacted suitable behavior. Whenever a person met another with courtesy, something like a reflection of the king appeared and functioned in the particular situation.

This is past and gone. The "divine right" king no longer exists. Where there is a king, he is limited. Our life is no longer in the form of an ascending and descending hierarchy, but it is all on a level, democratically structured, and increasingly so. This equality, felt and demanded everywhere, causes the earlier forms of courtesy to disappear. But mere leveling is chaos, and soon a dictatorship replaces the hierarchy, and force and violence take the place of reverence. But this is not really an order; it is simply force, and that means hidden chaos. This constantly breaks out in revolt, as long as reverence and a new kind of courtesy do not evolve from the democratic level.

But how can this come about?

I believe that it is possible only if we begin with the dignity of man, who must be honored, because there are forces which dishonor him and seek to violate his dignity. We need only recall the various forms of totalitarianism. But man must be honored in relation to Him who created man in His image and who requires us to honor this image. Here there is a reference to a higher level which remains in all equality and, indeed, alone makes this possible.

Another point of departure for the evolution of a new courtesy is the vulnerability of man, which requires that we should recognize our responsibility toward each other. What psychology, sociology, and biology tell us about man points out the necessity of this attitude. And not only that. They also show us the constantly increasing danger in which man finds himself in consequence of his economic and technical progress. This progress, upon which he prides himself, indicates an increasing artificiality of life and a consequent threat to life, to say nothing of the power which man has acquired over nature and human life. And no one knows how man, who is not wise or well anchored, but rather driven by every kind of passion, will use this power.

Therefore it is to be hoped that present-day man will become aware of a fellowship in danger and will carry out this awareness in mutual responsibility and consideration, which means courtesy.

There is also a courtesy in relation to God. We may consider, for example, that we cannot come to church improperly dressed; that there is a suitable attitude — both external and internal — for prayer; that all thought and speech related to God must be carried on in the proper disposition. Here the Liturgy can be our teacher: it is permeated with reverence. All that is spoken, heard, or done — every action — is, as it were, veiled in reverence, so that we may ever remain conscious of the mystery which is here carried out.

Then our meditation, if it is properly carried on, reaches a height which constitutes the ultimate mystery. Have we ever considered how God honors His creature? His whole attitude toward man rests upon the unfathomable fact that He created him free.

God, who is all-powerful, wills that man should be a free person, self-dependent, disposing of himself, and acting from an inner impulse. God does not force us or terrify us or mislead us, not even when man turns against God and thereby against himself. We hesitate to say that God is courteous. The word must be elevated to the summit of its significance before we can apply it to Him. The fact that He created freedom and continually preserves it is the inconceivable lordly courtesy which He shows to His creature.

But those who have grown into intimacy with God tell us in addition that God here shows a tenderness which is more overwhelming than His very omnipotence; indeed, it is perhaps only the converse of His perfect power.

Images reveal much, often more than concepts. But we must interpret them correctly. How meaningful it is when, in the New Testament, Christ's admonition that man should receive His message is expressed in this image: "Behold, I stand at the door and knock."[43] He who speaks in this way is He to whom "is given all power in Heaven and on earth,"[44] and who, "with a rod of iron," could shatter every obstacle "as one shatters a [useless] earthen vessel."[45]

[43]Rev. 3:20.
[44]Matt. 28:18.
[45]Rev. 2:27.

Gratitude

If the thought that we expressed at the beginning of our meditations is correct — that every virtue, in each case with some particular moral value as its dominant, expresses the whole man — then it must be true that history exerts its influence, on the life history of the individual as well as on the cultural development of a country or a nation. The same virtues do not always determine the moral attitude.

We might say that the virtues are like constellations which appear in certain epochs and govern the firmament of values and then gradually fade from our sight, giving room to others. This does not mean that they cease to be legitimate values. They still exercise an influence, because the epochs are not rigidly separated. Nevertheless, they no longer stand in the foreground of moral consciousness. Of course, they may later reappear as a result of the changes that take place in men's souls throughout the ages.

We shall now speak of one of these virtues, which, if I am not mistaken, is now receding, namely, the virtue of gratitude. Naturally we still give and receive whenever a person wishes to give pleasure to another or to help someone personally, but this has become a private matter, and even here we perceive a kind of organization of giving which is bound up with our business and consumer trade and which destroys spontaneity. We need only think of the mad rush of giving and receiving at Christmastime. No, what determines the general sentiment is not asking and giving but the announcement of rights and their satisfaction by means of organized associations. And the response is not gratitude but a receipt; then, the matter is properly settled.

This has certain great advantages — namely, that the matter is handled objectively, according to a properly conceived system, and personal feeling is not brought in where it does not really belong. The growing democratic consciousness of the personal dignity of all men also contributes to this; the feeling that what is a matter of proper economics cannot be left to individual requests and a gracious bestowing, but that social conditions must be met by a common effort. However, this brings with it the danger that the living element, that which the words *ask* and *thank, give* and *receive* mean, may disappear.

Even worse than this: there is danger that the image of a mechanical apparatus may become the criterion for human relations. Our society and its life appear as a structure of functions in which there is no question of asking and thanking, nor even of proper rights and duties, but merely of appropriate functioning. Insofar as this concept becomes dominant, there is, of course, no place for gratitude.

Let us attempt to obtain a view of this gradually disappearing virtue. Let us ask what is necessary so that gratitude may become possible.

Above all there is this: we can be grateful only to a person. Gratitude and petition are possible only between an "I" and a "thou." We cannot thank a law, a board, or a company. We may do so out of mere politeness when the proper sum is handed to us, in order to keep everything in the domain of good manners, but real gratitude does not enter into the matter, for gratitude is the expression of a personal encounter in human need.

But two persons, one of whom is situated so that he has something or can do something, while the other has not or cannot, stand face to face. The one asks, and the other is ready; the one gives, and the other thanks; and the two are united by a human tie. Here gratitude is possible, and it becomes a basis for community.

Furthermore, gratitude is possible only in the realm of freedom. For the fact that the sun rises in the morning or, to express it scientifically, that the earth comes into such a position in relation to the sun that it becomes visible: for this I am not grateful. It is certainly true that on a bright morning, very lively sentiments of gratitude may arise because something so powerful and beautiful is taking place. But these are the responses of man to Him who has created all, or else they are the after-effects of a time in which the sun itself was revered as a divinity. Otherwise, we know the astronomical formulas, and if we have proper intelligence, we know why the sun must "rise." I do not thank for that, nor for a machine that runs properly.

Here, too, there may be a transfer of feelings. If my car runs well under difficult conditions, I may feel about it as if it were a tried-and-true comrade. But in reality, there is no gratitude here. If a machine is properly constructed and properly handled, it must function properly.

Nor do I thank when I have a rightful claim upon something. If I have bought some article and it is delivered to me, I do not thank, but I give a receipt: "Such and such a thing received in good condition." If I have made an agreement on the basis of which another person must perform some service, I do not thank him afterward, but say, "It is right"; anything beyond this is mere politeness.

True gratitude can exist only in the realm of the voluntary. The more our attitude toward human affairs approaches our attitude toward mechanical functions — this board regulates traffic, another the conditions of labor; one thing must be done according to the law at this time, another thing at another time — the less room there will be for the free response of the heart which says, "I thank you." Its place is taken by the statement that says one has received his due.

A third condition necessary for gratitude is this: he who gives the gift must do so with reverence for the one who receives; otherwise he wounds the receiver's self-respect. He must not give with indifference; neither must he play the part of one who condescends; nor must he desire to show his power by the gift. A danger for all in social service is the desire to feel their power, for the person in need is, as such, weaker than the one who helps, and when he thanks for the assistance, he admits his weakness thereby.

All this makes gratitude difficult. If the one who helps lets the other feel his superiority, then gratitude dies and in its place we find humiliation and resentment. How many persons who receive would like to throw the gift into the giver's face!

So there are three important conditions. Gratitude can exist only between an "I" and a "thou." As soon as the consciousness of the personal quality disappears and the idea of the apparatus prevails, gratitude dies. Gratitude can exist only in the realm of freedom. As soon as there is a "must" or a claim, gratitude loses its meaning. Gratitude can exist only with reverence. If there is no mutual respect, gratitude perishes and turns to resentment. Anyone who gives assistance to others should think about that. Only the assistance which makes gratitude possible really deserves the name.

True asking and giving, true receiving and thanking are fine and are human in the deepest sense of the word. They are based upon the consciousness that we stand together in our need. Accidentally here and now, one person has something, the other does not; one person can and the other cannot. Tomorrow it may be the other way around.

But human need is not the only occasion which can give rise to gratitude. Gratitude can spring up wherever kindliness perceives an opportunity to bring joy or create beauty or brighten life. Then the one who is made joyful says, "You have done this. I thank you." This is a fine thing, and if it is really true that the structure of our life leaves less and less room for gratitude, then we should want to seek such opportunities wherever they exist, and create them whenever possible with that power which cannot be overcome, because it is the central power of the heart — love.

Here we wish to bring to the reader's attention something which, in the light of what we have been saying, seems like a paradox and perhaps is one. (How many paradoxes life contains!) It cannot be reduced to a formula. There are moments when we feel that we must thank someone simply because he *is* — not for doing something or other, but simply for being. Actually this is nonsense, because he did not make himself. And yet the feeling is there. Perhaps it is unconsciously directed toward God, because it is He who willed that this person should exist. But perhaps there is something more to it, for *to be* is a verb and denotes action. So the feeling may perhaps be directed toward an "achievement" which cannot be really understood or explained.

This type of gratitude takes on a new and mysterious meaning in relation to God. In the *Gloria* of the Mass, we say, "We give You thanks for Your great glory." Historians tell us that this thanking, in Latin *gratias agere*, belongs to high ceremonial language and is an expression of honor: "We render homage to You because of Your great power and majesty." That may be so, and yet it is more than a mere expression of honor. It is also proper to remember that it is impossible for God not to be, and so we really have no occasion to thank Him for being.

On Mount Horeb, when Moses asked Him His name, God replied that His name was "I am."[46] In the case of every finite being, the fact that it is not merely thought, but really exists, is something additional; in God, this is essential to His nature, and it would be quite proper to address Him as "You who are." All this is true, and yet, in the unutterable immensity of God's essential glory, there seems to be something which we may call the freedom of real being. It is as if He gave us the fact that He is; as if His very being were a grace that He bestows upon us;

[46]Exod. 3:14.

as if His being were an achievement which lies beyond all concepts, and for which man expresses a gratitude which would ravish him into ecstasy if he really experienced it. (We trust that the reader will not be offended by this thought which actually was intended only to indicate something beyond all comprehension.)

Giving and thanking, which lift man above the functioning of a machine or the instinct of animals, are really the echo of something divine. For the very fact that the world exists and embraces such inexhaustible profusion is not something self-evident; it *is* because it was willed; it is a deed and a work.

At present, there exists a concept which is in one way indispensable, in another a calamity; that is, the concept of nature, and here we use the word in its modern sense. It signifies the sum total of all that is directly perceived, the whole which is governed by universally valid laws as it is investigated by science. But then it transcends itself, stands in opposition to the faith of the past, and means the world as that self-evident entity in which we live and search and work, but about whose origin we do not think. Nature is simply that which is, which is as it is and cannot be otherwise. When people adopt this view, the noblest things die, because they live by the very fact that they are not self-evident, that they are born of freedom. The world is not "nature," but a "work," the work of God. It *is* because He conceived it in His mind and because He wishes it to *be* in the mystery of the freedom of His love.

Hence the world is the abiding gift of God to us. The fact that we ourselves *are* is an abiding gift of God to us. That we are as we are and can breathe and feel and work is by no means self-evident, but is worthy of adoring wonder. To know this is part of man's basic consciousness. Constantly to receive oneself from the hand of God, and to thank Him for this, belongs to the essential being of man, of the real man who is as he was meant to be. It is quite possible that I might not be, and that the world might not be. Nothing essential would be lacking: "only I," "only the world." For God is self-sufficient.

Perhaps this is really the basis of all piety: to know and to accept and to confess, "You are, O Lord, and You suffice. But You willed that I should be, and I thank You for it." This is a prayer that always sets us right. Let us try it, perhaps in the morning when we are fresh and rested; when we, as it were, receive ourselves anew after the absence of sleep: "Lord, how good it is that You willed that I should be! I thank You that You have permitted me to be!"

Then the false sense of self-evidence will be dissipated; the mechanism of our concept of nature and the presumptions of our pride will disintegrate. Everything between God and ourselves will come to life, and things will be right. Later, in the course of the day, they will again be hidden by the turmoil of wishes and events. But they *were* there in the morning, and they will be there again tomorrow morning and will bring order into our existence.

We may go a little farther in our meditation. What about God Himself? Does He thank? We might reply at once, "What could that mean? All things belong to Him." But if we want to know the mind of God, we should not sit down and cogitate how "the absolute Being" should act; we must ask God Himself. And there is a place where His heart is revealed, and that is in Christ.

Did Christ thank? When He sat beside the well in Samaria and asked the woman, "Give me to drink" and she drew the water and handed Him the vessel, He certainly would have thanked her.[47] Or when Lazarus and his sisters, Mary and Martha, entertained Him in the house at Bethany, He must have thanked them, in grace and power.[48]

And when the despised woman of Magdala came to the feast of Simon and poured the precious ointment over the feet of Jesus and, in the perfection of contrite humility, dried them with her hair, while the self-righteous Pharisee and the hypocritical Judas turned against her, Jesus spoke immortal words about her.[49] How mysteriously His knowledge of her repentance and the pardon of her sins are combined in His words with the fragrance of the ointment and the beauty of the gesture.

In Jesus we find gratitude in weakness and in power, for He had need of all things because He had become one of us and we, presumptuous as we are, have need of the gifts of existence from our first breath to our last. But Jesus responded by looking into the eyes of the one who showed Him a kindness and touching his heart.

Who can measure how much of this can be referred to God? Who knows — if we may speak in this way — what God feels when we do not merely perform our duty to Him, but give Him love; when our littleness strives to be generous toward Him? Then there is something in God which we may

[47]John 4:6-7.
[48]John 12:1-2.
[49]Luke 7:36-48.

faintly and distantly indicate by the word *gratitude*, very briefly, and then it plunges into mystery. But someday He will show us how He received our gift, and that will be a part of our blessedness.

Unselfishness

The name of the virtue which we are now going to consider is curious. If we examine it, it makes us wonder. What do unselfishness and its converse, selfishness, really mean?

How can we seek that which we are, our own self, or get away from that which is the basis of all that we are and do, and is even the basis of this very attempt to get away from it? Let us consider more carefully what this curious something is, the self, of which we speak in such strange fashion.

The "self" of a person may mean simply the piece of reality that he is — he, man, in distinction from a tree or an animal; he, this man, in distinction from anyone else and from all other men. That definition of self would be correct, but would still remain something external, statistical.

We must delve more deeply. Then self means the particular characteristic quality of the person: his peculiarities, talents, possibilities, and also his limitations, failings, and faults — all these gathered into one around a central point, namely, himself. So then, self would be what we call "personality." This would be richer and more decided as the qualities are more developed, more clearly defined, more harmonious, and as the

151

whole is stronger and more efficient. From this point of view, we speak of a great or mediocre or small personality, strong or weak, genuine or false, and so on.

In an even deeper sense, self means the curious fact that this being, called a man, not only exists but possesses himself. How does he possess himself? Especially by knowing about himself. No animal, however noble, knows about itself. A man knows that he is. He knows his possibilities and weaknesses, at least some of them, because daily experience presents them to his consciousness. He is able to know them better and better if he makes the effort, because he can observe and understand himself, can examine and judge himself. He can ask, "Why did I do this in this way and not in another? Was it right or wrong?" In doing this, he grasps himself and possesses himself in his mind. Sometimes when his work is successful or he feels the surging of life, he rejoices in thinking, "This was granted to me; I am allowed to be this."

This involves something more, or at least the possibility of something. "Being oneself" means that man can dispose of himself. We experience this when we reflect in some situation, "What shall I do — this or that?" And finally we decide, "I shall do that." In this decision, man disposes of himself, de-cides for himself. He is not merely moved from without as a stone is moved by a force stronger than its own weight, but he is activated from within. He is not compelled from within as an animal is compelled by its instincts, but he determines himself from some point which lies deeper than all which belongs to his immediate being: organs, urges, talents, and dispositions. We could say it lies higher than all these — freedom. Because he is able to do this, he has power over his actions. He can also work on himself, can curtail certain qualities and strengthen others, and in this way, change the relations of the different elements of his nature to each other. In short, he can do all that we call the formation of self, or self-education.

It has been maintained many times and is still being maintained that such freedom does not exist. At the moment when we hear the objection, it impresses us. But as soon as we come to our senses, we know that it is in error. Freedom does exist. We are free. We are not always free; frequently, we are not entirely so; but, basically and potentially, we are often really so.

Certainly various elements influence our decisions: heredity, disposition, environment, the particular situation, urges, physical and mental conditions, and the like. But all these only supply the ground on which freedom makes the decision. And it does really decide. And even if circumstances should prevent the carrying out of the decision, it still exists as the basic possibility and standard and gives to the whole event its particular — and sometimes very bitter — character.

Certainly all that happens has its reason, even a free decision. We can always ask, "Why do you do this?" and we receive the answer, "For this or that reason." Therefore, the objector might say, we cannot speak of freedom. But here the reason, or rather the motive, is confused with the cause. The motive of the decision is always some particular purpose or intention, but the decision is its own cause. It is the primary power, the initiative.

Apart from such considerations, the freedom reveals itself in an interior echo, in conscience, in the consciousness of responsibility for the action. It is a strange and mysterious phenomenon that an interior feeling says not only, "That was harmful," or, "That was dangerous," but, "That was wrong; you should not have done that, and yet you did it. Now it belongs to you, and you must answer for it before the laws of good and evil; not another, but you." Here, in the sense of responsibility, the self is revealed in its ineffaceable austerity.

Of course, much more could be said on the subject from the standpoint of logic, psychology, sociology, and so on. Discussions about freedom are endless. Here our purpose was only to make clear the meaning of the word, so that we might understand what is indicated by the terms *selfishness* and *unselfishness*, namely, the manner in which a person is himself and how he possesses himself; what attitude he assumes and what intention directs him.

A man may have a task to do, something demanded by his vocation. He can do it with his eye upon himself, upon the impression he will make upon others, the advantages which will accrue to him, and so on. If that is the case, he has been seeking himself in his work. As far as the work is concerned, it has probably been done badly, or at least not as well as it might have been. And that upon which his eye was fixed, his self, has not fared very well in the process; for keeping our eyes upon ourself makes us crooked, and paying attention to the impression produced deprives us of genuineness. To be unselfish here would mean as much as to be objective, to fix one's attention upon the task and not to think of oneself; to do the work correctly and properly, as it should be done. Then the work flourishes, for the person doing it is concerned with the task, not with his vain self. In addition — and this is what concerns us particularly here — such an attitude produces a singularly free mental area in which the person really becomes himself.

Here we touch something strange that must lead every serious-minded person to deeper reflection, namely, the paradox of the person. As soon as the person fixes his eye upon himself, he fills the mental space, so to speak, in which a portion of life is to take place; he gets in the way of his own realization. But if he forgets himself and turns his attention simply to the matter in hand, the space opens out, and now the person truly becomes himself.

A large number of our daily acts consist in coming into relation with another person; they are "I-thou" relationships. But these can be carried on in very different ways. Encounters in friendship and in society, collaboration in our profession or business, helping the needy: in all these, we can behave in such a way that we play a part, and we often do this. We watch to see what impression we are making, whether the other esteems us properly, whether we shall receive something when we give, and so on.

But what happens? The living "I-thou" relationship withers; that which should be a clear face-to-face encounter follows two different lines which interfere with each other; it becomes broken, crooked. And the other perceives this. He thinks, "That person is not really with me; he is always thinking of himself." And this makes him uncertain. He does not reach a straightforward, confident "thou" relation, but he becomes suspicious.

But the man who is open: in his friendliness, disinterested in showing honor, straightforward in giving help, he departs from himself, but by that very fact, his true self arises free and harmonious from its inner depths and calls to the self of the other.

Herein we find the mysterious dialectic of the person: the more a person seeks himself, the more he slips away from himself. The more important he considers himself, the more insignificant he becomes. The vain, calculating person who lives only for himself thinks that he is attaining a fuller, stronger selfhood. In reality, he is becoming interiorly crippled because he never moves in that free space which only unselfishness creates. As we depart from ourself and give our attention to the other, to the work, or to the task, the true self awakens and grows. A person is more truly himself the more freely he leaves himself for the other person with whom he is dealing or for the task that confronts him.

Of course, he must also pay attention to himself. He must examine himself to know whether he has done the right thing, has been wise in his dealings with others, and has served the purpose of his calling or profession. He must make the many corrections which life requires, because otherwise there will be ill feeling, annoyance, and harm. But the essential attitude of man is the movement away from himself toward the other person and toward the task to be accomplished.

The same rule can also be applied in religion. There is selfishness and unselfishness toward God. Jesus said, "Not as I will but as Thou wilt."[50] This word cuts a sharp line between the will that seeks the self and that which seeks the Father. To the extent to which man seeks God, he moves away from himself to the divine Thou; but this is not so that he will lose

[50]Matt. 26:39.

himself; no, he truly finds himself in God. This is the promise that the Lord has given, saying, "He that finds his life shall lose it, and he that shall lose his life for me shall find it."[51] This refers, first of all, to the losing of one's life in martyrdom. But the Greek word for *life*, *psyche*, in the New Testament also means the soul and its eternal life. Whenever a person, in opposition to God, clings to his soul, he loses it, but when he gives it to God, he finds it. Man gives his soul to God in every act of obedience to God's holy will and, at the same moment, God gives it back to him, and the soul has become more truly itself than it was before.

A mysterious exchange between man and God! The more often man does this, the more his life advances, in this constant giving of himself and receiving himself again from the hand of God, the more he becomes the person he should be or, we might say, becomes the person he truly is.

The mystics speak of the "birth of God in man." This is a mysterious phrase about whose ultimate meaning we shall not speak here, but one thing we can understand immediately: God wishes to enter into man, to find a place in him and assume a human form, here in this person who is generically one among countless others, but personally is unique; that is, he is himself.

There is a resemblance to God in all things. Everything expresses Him, each according to its own kind, and this expression of God constitutes its basic created nature. But God wishes to express Himself in man in a special way, in each person according to his particular character. This is the inmost

[51]Matt. 10:39.

core of what we call "personality," a reflection — if we may be permitted this comparison — of the Incarnation of the eternal Son. The real, essential Incarnation took place in Christ, but by His grace, which confers His image, God wishes to enter into every person and express Himself in him, and in everyone in a special and unique manner. Every believer should be an expression of God. The foundation is laid in Baptism, in the "new birth of water and the Holy Spirit," as we learn from the nocturnal conversation of the Lord with Nicodemus.[52] And every act of the believer in doing the will of God constitutes a step in that direction.

The perfection of the expression can be seen in the saints. God "appears" in them. But since man is the image of God, and God is the model of man, this manifestation also reveals the essential nature of man, of every man. He becomes truly himself. How did St. Francis of Assisi become truly himself? By not seeking himself in anything. If he had remained the son of Bernardone and continued to play the great role in Assisi and Umbria, which his father wished him to play, and for which his talents and his fortune fitted him, then he would probably have been a glamorous and charming person, but his essential nature would have remained hidden. But when he took his great step — "Only God and nothing else" — then the beauty of God blossomed in him, and he became the man he was meant to be, the man who expressed the magnanimity of divine love more than almost anyone else.

Every saint reflects in a particular way the Incarnation of God in Christ. In no longer seeking himself, he gives place to

[52] John 3:5.

God, who makes him the person he really should be, as God's essential Incarnation in Christ manifested what man as such, the "son of man" really is. Of course, the way thereto is a self-surrender, one sacrifice after another, the "painful death of self" as the spiritual masters call it.

Every virtue has its model in God. All virtues are modes in which God's goodness is reflected in man in particular respects. This is also true of unselfishness, however strange this statement may sound at first.

Before and above all, God is infinitely Himself. When Moses on Mount Horeb asked Him His name, so that His message might be ratified among the horde of pagan gods of that time, God answered, "I am the 'I am.' "[53] Thereby He expressed His eternal selfhood, and all who seriously meditate about God must learn from this word if they are not to go astray. The word says there is no name which can express God from the point of view of finite beings; that is, classify Him with anything known and created. His name is "He," or, to put it in another way, "That it is so" — this is God's name.

But the letter to the Philippians says of the Son of God, that is, of God Himself, "Let nothing be done through contention, neither by vainglory, but in humility let each esteem others better than himself; each one not considering the things that are his own, but those that are other men's. For let this mind be in you, which was also in Christ Jesus, who being in the form of God, thought it not robbery to be equal with God, but emptied Himself, taking the form of a servant, being made in the likeness of men, and in habit found as a man. He

[53]Cf. Exod. 3:14.

humbled Himself, becoming obedient unto death, even to the death of the Cross. For which cause God also hath exalted Him and hath given Him a name which is above all names; that in the name of Jesus, every knee should bow, of those that are in Heaven, on earth, and under the earth; and that every tongue should confess that the Lord Jesus Christ is in the glory of God the Father."[54]

Something tremendous is expressed in this passage: that the Son of God did not anxiously and forcefully cling to His eternal selfhood, as to something unlawfully acquired, but "emptied" Himself, or more exactly "annihilated" Himself, and gave up His selfhood by becoming a servant, although He was the Lord of all. He became a servant, a bondslave, in bitter earnest, even to the death on the cross, which a malefactor had to suffer. But thereby he obtained the new "name," the name *Christ*, the anointed and victorious one, and *Kyrios*, the Lord God, who is enthroned above all creation; and this brings eternal glory to the Father.

It is an ineffable mystery that God does this, is able to do this and yet remain God. Revelation tells us that God acts in this way and that it is glorious for Him to do so. A God who acted, thought, and willed otherwise cannot exist. He would be, as Pascal[55] says, a "god of the philosophers," a concept of God by which man seeks to justify his own self-centeredness.

God is sovereignly unselfish, and every act of unselfishness in man faintly reflects this divine mystery.

[54]Phil. 2:3-11.

[55]Blaise Pascal (1623-1662), French theologian, mathematician, and physicist.

Recollection

An expression which was familiar to the religious and ethical language of the past, but which is seldom used in our day, is *recollection*. And yet that which it denotes is more relevant to us today. Psychiatrists and educators in particular are beginning to understand its significance. So the thoughts of this reflection will find quite a few points of contact.

To have a better understanding of what *recollection* means, let us recall the structure of our existence. It oscillates between two poles which are related to those mentioned in the chapter on silence and speech. The first pole is the interiority of the person, his center. It would not be easy to explain what this center is, but everyone who uses the word of himself knows what he means: the point of inward relation, that which makes of his powers, his characteristics, his attitudes, and his actions, not a confused chaos, but a unity. That is one pole.

The other is the connection of external things, events, circumstances, and relations; it is the other persons, their way of life, and their actions — history. In short, it is the world insofar as the individual has the power to survey it and the ability to experience it.

Learning the Virtues

Between these two poles, the center in us and the world about us, our life moves. I constantly go out of myself to the objects around me; I observe, grasp, take possession, fashion, and arrange. Then I return to my center and ask myself, "What is that? Why is it so? What does it resemble, and how does it differ? Wherein does its essence consist?" Here, in knowledge, that which I have experienced outside is perfected.

If I want to do something, I do not simply work at random, but I consider its purpose and what the situation demands. I make a decision, and only then do I have direction and order for my activity "outside."

After I have acted, I reconsider and test my action. Did I do things right? Was I just to the person involved? Have I done my duty?

What we have said simplifies the matter. Actually, the "out" and "back," and "out" and "back" again, takes place not only once, but countless times. It is a constant play of acts which make up our daily life.

So the two areas are related to each other. What happens outside is guided and judged by that which is within; what is within is called, aroused, and fed by what is without. If we ask ourselves what person is to be considered properly developed in this respect, the answer must be: he in whose life these two poles function in proper relation to each other; the person who does not lose his direction in outward matters nor become entangled with himself, but in whose life the two areas are well balanced and determine and perfect each other.

But in our ordinary experience, it is different. Here the objects of exterior life predominate most powerfully. Their many forms — the insistence of their qualities; the tasks which they impose upon us; their value, which arouses our desire; their danger, which awakens fear — are so powerful that they gain the preponderance and draw our life outward. So we have the extroverted person, whose inner self is weak and becomes constantly weaker.

On the whole, this has long been the case, and those concerned about the deeper culture of man have long warned us. But the condition has become especially dangerous at present, because the stimuli which force themselves upon man have become so strong and so numerous, and their strength and number is constantly increasing. Man is in constant turmoil, not only in systems which catch and absorb him, but generally in a chaos that he cannot grasp.

Moreover, the publicizing of existence has increased to an alarming extent. Events are announced with increasing speed and completeness — so immediately that one is tempted to say that the account is a part of the event, and that the latter takes place from the outset before the lenses and microphones of the announcers. Publicity forces itself upon men's personal lives without the least consideration, so that privacy is plainly disappearing. The boundaries of life's course become transparent as glass, and men move behind them like fish in an aquarium, whose activities one can observe from all sides.

It is very symbolic that the modern house frequently has no wall.[56] Within the house, man lives as if he were outside and imagines that this makes him free. Actually the inner world evaporates. And as if this were not enough, the outer world is

[56]The author is most likely referring to the replacement of walls with plate-glass windows, seen most frequently in modern skyscrapers, but also found in many designer homes. — ED.

Learning the Virtues

expressly brought in. We all know homes in which it is never quiet because the radio is constantly blaring away, or television brings the sensation of world events into the hours when persons should be by themselves.

So we have the man who no longer has a living center. The events of life constantly flow through him and carry him out. He feels cramped if he is in his room; he must always be in motion. He cannot manage to stay alone; he must always have people around him. To spend an evening quietly with a book would seem to him a waste of time, because he must always be "doing something." The request to consider his own life eye to eye with himself, to think about encounters, activities, responsibilities, and principles: this would embarrass him. He would not know how to go about it and, after the briefest reflection, would slip away from himself. Or even worse: he would not want to see himself at all.

The life of such a man resolves itself into reactions to external stimuli. He does not stand anywhere, but is tossed about by a thousand influences. He does not possess himself, but "happens" anywhere. He has no convictions, but only views which have come to him from newspapers and radio. He does not act from interior initiative, but only as he is propelled by impulses that come from without.

This has a special significance in our religious life. What is the core of all piety? It is the consciousness of the reality of God; that He "is," is living here and now, and is working, acting, and ruling. This idea develops further and becomes the consciousness that actually God alone is primarily and originally real and that all finite creation is only "through Him" and "before Him"; that He alone works and acts in a sovereign creative manner, and we can work only in Him. Piety means living in the sight of God.

But there is more. Piety means a dialogue with God and, above all, the fact that one addresses Him. But in reality, to whom does one speak in addressing God? Usually to a fog — or only to oneself without the consciousness of a Thou. If we are speaking to a man, we look into his eyes, we note his expression, so that we know that our words are addressed to a countenance and beyond that to what is expressed thereby: the mind that thinks, the heart that feels, the person who exists. In his countenance I read what is there expressed, the person himself. For the act of addressing God, the psalmists use the expression "to seek the face of God,"[57] to speak to the countenance of God. But how is that done?

Piety means seeking the face of God, and living according to His countenance. This is a part of the meaning of creation, as St. Augustine said, "Thou hast made us for Thyself, O God."[58]

But we can do this only if we are at home with ourselves, masters of ourselves. We can do this only if the inner realm is open and the other person becomes clear, or at least the fact that we are addressing Him becomes clear. In the exterior world in which we usually find ourselves, in the turmoil which pervades our being, God is, so to speak, wiped out. The many images of things, the many countenances of men prevent the countenance of God — this mysterious entity which all who

[57]Cf. Ps. 23:6 (RSV = Ps. 24:6).
[58]St. Augustine (Bishop of Hippo and Doctor of the Church; 354-430), *Confessions*, Bk. 1, ch. 1.

associate with God know — from being clear, from being perceived.

But up to this point, we have only an attention, a direction on the part of man, not a dialogue. For this we need the other voice, the voice of God. Indeed, this comes first — and only so do we grasp the matter rightly. For we can address God only if He permits it; we can speak the word only if He releases it within us.

But how does God speak within us? And how does He enable us to understand His word and to answer it with ours. His voice and our hearing and answering we call "conscience." This is a wonderful thing. Constantly, we are touched by the call which comes to us from the good, the right, that which is worthy of being and *should* be. This good is all-inclusive and yet quite simple. It constantly urges us, "Do me. Realize me. Carry me into the world so that the kingdom of the good may come into being." And let us assume that a voice within us, our conscience, replies, "Yes, I will, but how shall I do this?" And thereupon follows a silence, for the good is as unlimited in content as it is simple in form, and so it cannot simply be "done."

But then "the situation" takes shape; perhaps it has already done so and waits for us. It is like this: the stream of temporal things constantly flows around us. But again and again, objects, relations, and events form an image — this room, this person, this conversation, this need — and we are facing it. In this image, the good takes form as that which is here and now demanded. This turns to me, regards me, and addresses me, "Do this — here, now!" And conscience is the ability to perceive the call, to understand, and to decide: "Yes, I will!"

All this may be understood in a purely ethical way. Then it means the consciousness of always being bound by the moral law and the ability in each case to understand that law through the concrete situation. But the core of the whole matter is the religious relation. For "the good," in the final analysis, is God, His holiness; and the challenge to bring about the realization of the good in the world is His voice. But He demands of us that we bring into existence the kingdom of the good, His kingdom, in the world at the place where we are, hour by hour, according to the situation which always arises through Him, through His action and guidance, through His Providence.

The sensitivity to this constant admonition of the good, the ability to recognize the given hour as the elucidation of its commandment and the necessary assumption for its realization, and to grasp it by the readiness of true obedience and by confidence in our own interpretation and decision: all this is possible only as the result of an interior disposition which signifies attention and readiness; that means a standing before God, and this is recollection.

Only a recollected person recognizes the "hour," whether it has a great significance — the greatest was that of which the New Testament speaks in the words "The time is fulfilled"[59] — or whether it has a simpler one, for instance, that a decision upon which much depends should be rightly made. And there is also the everyday significance, that every hour of our life has its meaning for the kingdom of God. All this is possible only through an interior disposition which we call "recollection."

[59]Mark 1:15.

Learning the Virtues

From this point our thought continues: The whole existence of man takes place in the "I-Thou" relationship between
God and him. Things were created by the command of God.
"He spoke, and they were there,"[60] says the psalmist of the
constellations, and they exist through this command which
preserves them in being and reality. With man, it is different.
The account of creation expresses the special quality of the
creation of man by the marvelous figure of God bowing down
over the clay that had been formed into a human body and
breathing into it the life-giving element. This means that man
was created not as a species, but as an individual, and was so
regarded by God. God created him for the "I-Thou" relationship with Himself. So man's life goes on as a constant dialogue.
Through everything that occurs, and also through every movement of his own life, God speaks to him. We may say that the
life of faith consists in learning to carry on this dialogue, in
bringing all that happens to us and all that we do into this
dialogue, understanding it all in relation to God, and carrying
it out for Him.

But how can this be possible if man is in a constant state of
distraction, always extroverted, pulled this way and that by the
impressions that importune him? He can sustain this existence
in dialogue only if he is interiorly alive, if he is attentive,
listening — and listening in such a way that he goes on to
action, to obedience. In truth, man carries out the basic nature
of his existence only in the measure in which he is recollected.

What we have said of the "I-Thou" relation to God holds
true to a lesser degree of man's relation to another man. For

---

[60]Ps. 148:5.

some time, the point has been emphasized that our life is based upon a constant realization of the "I-thou" relation to another. We are conscious of the fact that the great danger of our age of masses and machines consists in making man a mere thing. We notice that the act of recognizing a person is different from that of recognizing a thing. In the case of the thing, we say "that over there"; in the case of a person, "you over there." Herein the meaning of what we call the person is revealed: a being that has been given freedom. From the "I-thou" relation comes the proper attitude of one man to another: reverence, faithfulness, and charity.

But this is possible only through recollection. The person who is not recollected treats men as if they were things. He counts them, groups them by catchwords, uses them for his purposes, and expends them. Only when the peculiar interior watchfulness, the particular attention which we call "recollection," comes into being is it possible to meet man as man. But the danger of not doing this, and hence the necessity of recognizing the problem, grows as the number of human beings grows and as our lives are in consequence determined more and more by machines, which treat all that they handle as mere things.

We must go on once more. Even the work of man — more precisely, the nobler work — can be understood only through recollection. How can we grasp the peculiar nature of a work of art if not by a kind of reflection of the "I-thou" relation? How does the manner in which a true connoisseur experiences a work of art differ from the manner in which a dealer rates it according to its market value? Evidently in an attention, a reverence, which is possible only as a result of recollection.

Learning the Virtues

Of course, this takes an effort. We need only to notice how people behave at an exhibition or a concert. Most of them do not establish a true relation to the work, but they treat it as a thing. We perceive this in the rapidity with which they become critics, comparing and evaluating, and this means that they take the work of art as an object. Here, too, recollection is essential, and we can tell by the face of the observer or listener whether he is capable of it and willing to make the effort.

Perhaps we would need to go a step farther and say that nature also can be met properly only if we approach it with some degree of recollection. How does the glance of a person who beholds in a tree the mystery of silent life without power of locomotion, uniting the depth of the earth, the breadth of space, and the height of heaven, differ from the glance of the woodman who looks to see if the tree should be felled, or the glance of the dealer who calculates its price in the market?

We might say the same thing of every form of nature. And the greatest danger of our age, with its mass tourism and recreation, which has become a business, consists in the fact that the attitude of recollection becomes more and more rare.

Let us return to the thought upon which we touched at the beginning of our meditation: the virtue of recollection means that a person has learned through natural disposition, education, and experience how life moves between the interior realm of personality and the exterior realm of the world, between the deep center and the far-reaching whole. It means that he has to some extent mastered the distraction and exteriorization of which we have spoken and has learned to set his inner self free and make it work effectively.

Recollection

This task has at all times led men to construct a definite, very strict type of life, the life of the hermit or the monk. Both of these words mean the same thing etymologically: a person who wants to find the essential thing, wants it so much that he wants nothing else. Therefore he leaves everything else and turns wholly to the interior realm, either as a hermit, one actually dwelling alone, or as a monk who dwells with others, but in a community whose rule guarantees a maximum of solitude. He withdraws his attention, his inclinations, and his powers from the world and gathers them within himself. He turns his attention increasingly toward God, dwelling within Him, and accustoms himself to stand before the face of God and to listen to His word.

We cannot do this, for we live in the world and have our tasks. We have various ties and obligations that bind us. But we, too, must learn to be at home within our interior center; otherwise we are distracted persons.

This cannot be done without effort, without serious and continued practice; it requires asceticism. This word — of which we have already spoken — originally meant simply "practice." But practice means that we arouse a dormant power, develop an organ which is undeveloped, put off a bad habit and form a good one, and so on.

Perhaps we refrain from going out, even though we are inclined to do so, and we attempt to "come to ourself" by means of quiet work, a book, or honest reflection — but without artificiality or trifling, soberly and earnestly. And if there is no quiet place at home or we have no room of our own, we go into a church, sit down, and find solitude. Or we do not permit the noisy radio to disturb the silence with its blaring, but we turn it off. We resist the impulse to turn on the television and to be at its mercy for hours. Instead we read something sensible. The same thing holds true of the newspapers, that mass of sensation, indiscretion, and shamelessness. We refuse to be taken over by these, even if only for a quarter of an hour. When we go along the street, all the attractions of the age press upon us: traffic, noise, people, advertisements, and display windows and their wares on exhibit. From all sides things call us, draw us, and take us away from ourselves. What an important practice it is to resist all this, not to let ourselves be torn to pieces, but to remain calm and self-possessed, and so on.

Man — and especially in our time — always wants to go to others, to speak, to hear, and to participate. He constantly wants to see something and wants something to be happening. This desire has become a mania, and if it is not fulfilled, he becomes restless and something drives him out. He who has realized what a valuable thing it is to be recollected must overcome this tendency — or let us speak more modestly, must strive to overcome it more and more. It is really a mania, and overcoming a mania is difficult, because the urge has affected the nerves. It takes a long time for it to cease, but it can be reduced to a proper measure.

But at the same time, something positive must be done; we must become established in the interior world, must be ourselves and be interiorly independent. What we have been saying must not be taken as a moral sermon, but realistically, as spoken from experience, as pointing out the way to a rewarding life. For distraction, the constant outward motion, makes for an interior emptiness. If we try to imagine the end to which this scattered life leads, the thought occurs to us that the end will be a hopeless boredom interrupted by outbreaks of desperate impatience. So we must resist, for the sake of life itself, that it may have meaning.

This can be attained only by constantly examining ourselves: "How was it today? Did I possess my soul? Or was I in a constant state of agitation? Is my life such that I cannot attain self-possession? What must be changed?" And we must do this seriously, not with that dishonest resignation which gives up because it really does not want things to be different.

Then — and above all — we must seek the face of God, must realize what is the basic truth of our existence. God is the Eternally Existent One, the only one who lives from and through Himself. He is here. He is "the One Who Is." But we are and exist through Him; we are here before Him; we are ourselves only because He wills us to be.

This "He and I," "I before Him," "I through Him"; this hearkening to His word; this seeking and speaking, "Thou, God": this is what makes us interiorly alive and firm.

This interiority is the counterbalance to the mass of things, the multitude of people, and the turmoil of external events — to publicity, fashion, and advertising. It is also — and after the experiences of the past half-century, we must emphasize this — the only true counterbalance to the violence of the state, the modern, rationalistic, technological state which is always in danger of becoming an ochlocracy and hence totalitarian, and which must deprive man of self and of interiority in order to have dominion over him.

Revelation tells us that man is the image of God. Therefore God is man's original model and His being opens for us — in the manner permitted to our thought — a way to Him. But we can say that He is most perfectly recollected; completely unified; entirely self-possessed; living, feeling, and knowing Himself through and through.

In the history of occidental metaphysics, we find an attempt to approach the nature of mind or spirit, which states that each being is higher in rank, the richer and yet the simpler it is. The spirit is decisively simple since it cannot be divided, but it is articulated by its various acts and their relation in time, by its relation to the body which it animates and the objects to which it turns.

The sovereign spirit, God, is perfectly simple. He contains within Himself the fullness of life in the pure simplicity of being. He is entirely recollected, at one with Himself and therefore perfectly master of Himself and completely happy.

Silence

The life of man is passed between silence and speech, stillness and the word — two poles which are related to those which we considered in the reflection on recollection.

We sometimes say the word is spiritual, but that is not the case. It is human. In it that union of matter and spirit which we call man reaches its highest refinement. By the tone which the breath produces through the movements of throat and chest, the speaker expresses his interior meaning. At first he has this within himself; he thinks it and feels it. But it is hidden. Then he projects it into the figure made up of tone and sound, and thereby it is revealed to the hearer. The latter understands what the speaker means; he can answer, and so a conversation ensues. This is a wondrous thing, a great mystery. He who could understand it would understand man.

We must not let this be destroyed by naturalistic platitudes which seek to derive the word from the cry of an animal. This cry may express quite directly fear or pain or enticement or whatever it may be, but for all that, it is not a word. This comes into being only when the sound-structure communicates a meaning which was first thought — a truth. But only man is capable of this, for only in him is there a personal spirit. If an animal that lives with man seems to do something of this sort, that is a misapprehension on our part. What the animal produces is not a communication but an expression, often quite complicated. Only a man can put into the movements of the sound a truth of life, of science, of piety.

The word is one basic form of human life; silence is the other, and it is as great a mystery. Silence does not mean only that no word is spoken and no sound is uttered. This alone does not signify silence; the animal is capable of this, and the rock even more so. Rather, silence is that which takes place when man, after speaking, returns to himself and grows still; or when he who could speak remains still. Only he who can speak can be silent. Silence means that he who would "go forth" by speaking remains in inner reserve; it is a knowing, a feeling, a living stillness, a vibrating within itself.

The two things belong together. Only he who is also able to be silent can speak meaningfully; otherwise he talks nonsense. Only he who can also speak can properly keep silence; otherwise he is dumb. Man lives in these two mysteries; their unity expresses his nature.

To be capable of silence is a virtue. He who does not know how to keep silence does the same thing with his life as a man who would wish only to exhale and not to inhale. We need only imagine this to feel terrified. The man who is never silent dissipates his humanity.

As we have already said, in speech the inner man is revealed. What I think, feel, or intend is known only to me. But as soon as I express it in words, it becomes known. It stands in space between me — the speaker — and the other who hears it. Thereby I give the hearer a share in what I possess interiorly.

Many conflicts are resolved by being brought out into the open by means of words. But there are also experiences which should not be revealed. When someone has performed an act of magnanimity or delicacy, he knows that if he spoke of it, it would disintegrate. Therefore he veils it in silence and keeps it to himself. And if, in some dark hour, he must ask himself if life is worthwhile, then the act comes to his attention and justifies his existence.

Through speech we have communion. When two persons exchange views about something, the word passes back and forth between them. Question and answer, affirmation and objection move onward toward clarity and probe more deeply until the moment comes when they know, "So it is!" Now they have communion in truth, a marvelous manner of sharing.

There are also times in which man does not desire communion, does not need another to share the truth that is inwardly beheld. It may be that one enters a church, in which the presence of God may be perceived. One sits down, is conscious of the pillars rising round about, feels the vast space, notes the sacred images, and silence fills the soul. What is brought to our awareness at such times must not be put into words. If we tried to express it, something would be lost.

By speech man enters into history. He faces a situation in which something must be decided and asks himself what should be done. If he decides and expresses his decision, then history begins. For the word has weight; we are responsible for it. It is power; it sets cause and effect in motion, and man himself is affected by it.

But if he does not wish to enter into history, then he is silent and thereby withdraws into the realm of reserve.

We could mention various other things. The most important events of human life take place between these two poles of existence. But usually there are not two poles, but one, and consequently no pole at all, since a pole requires its contrary in order to function. Usually speech is the predominant thing, since man cannot be silent, or rather does not wish to be; for if he is truly silent, he comes to himself, and to be with himself is something he finds unendurable. He then perceives all that is stunted, perplexed, and spoiled in himself, and he runs away from himself into speech.

Only in silence is true knowledge attained. This does not mean cognizance. This, too, is good and necessary. For instance, it may establish the fact that a certain person is ill and in pain. Then we can act accordingly, can apply remedies or call a physician, and then the matter is taken care of. But the desire for knowledge asks, "What is pain? What does it bring about in our existence when it is interiorly accepted, lived, or rejected? And what of this person? What effect does pain have on his life?" These are questions which do not find their answer in speech. Perhaps they find an external answer but certainly not the answer of an interior understanding which grasps the essential thing. The person who is speaking misses the very point, the interior vis-à-vis, the penetrating glance into the existence before him, the understanding of the way in which this one unique existence functions.

In order to attain this, we must recollect ourselves, become silent, bring the matter before our interior sight, and enter into the other person's feelings. Then, at the proper time, we begin to understand what is taking place in the person who suffers. This is knowledge, the dawning of truth. He who cannot be silent never has this experience.

What holds true of knowledge also holds true of our associations. Association with others consists largely in giving to them something of oneself: friendliness, helpfulness, one's presence, and finally the joy of complete communion. But can one give something of himself if he does not possess himself? He who is always speaking does not really possess himself, for he always slips away from himself, and what he gives to others, when he should give himself, is nothing but words.

And finally, only in silence do we attain the presence of God. This is so true that building one's whole existence upon silence has become a form of life. There are religious orders that do this. It is a daring enterprise, which, if it is properly carried out, leads far into the silent kingdom of God. But it may become dangerous if generosity and wisdom are lacking. We shall not go into that, however, but shall keep to ordinary life.

The beginning of all religious life is the awareness that God is. He is not merely a feeling or an idea, but a reality. He is more real than I am myself; He is the essential, self-based, eternal reality, and all serious religious life leads to the experience that God is and we are only before Him and through Him. But God is not only real; He is "somebody," Himself. We have already spoken in these meditations of the way in which Scripture expresses this. Scripture speaks of His countenance. "Show us, O Lord, Thy countenance, and we shall be healed," says the psalmist.[61]

[61]Ps. 79:4 (RSV = Ps. 80:3).

179

Learning the Virtues

Are we familiar with this experience? Do we have knowledge of the countenance of God? Do we know what it means when the Scripture says that God turns to me, He looks upon me, and He takes account of me? Only when we do can we properly and meaningfully say, "Thou, God."

Have we ever thought how wonderful it is that I can really say "Thou" to God? That He is even the essential Thou for me — so much so that a man in prayer could be told, "God and thy soul, nothing else in the world"? And when he asked, "Lord, what of the others?" the reply was, "It holds true of everyone, God and he, nothing else."

Into this most intimate relation — God and I — we do not come by speaking, but only by silence; when we are recollected, our inmost soul is opened and the sacred presence can manifest itself.

This silence must be learned. No virtue comes to us spontaneously. There are predispositions. There is the introverted person in contrast to the one who is predominantly extroverted. But this predisposition does not suffice. It may make a person thoughtful, attentive to the processes of his own mind, serious, perhaps even melancholy; but all this is fluctuating, subject to the moods and experiences of the moment, and can be thwarted and confused by external events.

So we must take pains. We must resist the endless chatter and noise that fills the world; we must struggle as an asthmatic person struggles for breath. Otherwise something in us withers and dies.

But the external noise is only half the problem and perhaps not even the most difficult half. The other is the inner turmoil, the whirl of thoughts, the drive of desire, the restlessness and worries of the mind, the burden of care, the wall of dullness, or whatever it may be which fills our interior world as the rubble fills an abandoned well.

We must be serious about this. A life properly lived includes practice in silence. This begins with keeping our mouth shut whenever this is required by the confidence of another person, the duties of our vocation, tact, or respect for others. It goes on to include keeping silence at times even when it might be permissible to speak, especially if speaking would create an impression. Not to speak at such times is a good exercise in keeping our mastery over the inordinate desire to talk. We should strive to conquer the mania for constant chatter and idle talk. How many superfluous things we say in the course of the day — how many foolish things! We must learn that silence is beautiful, that it is not emptiness, but true and full life.

And then, in addition, we must learn interior stillness, lingering over a serious problem, an important task, or the thought of a person whom we value. In doing this we shall make a great discovery: that the interior world of man is spacious and admits of ever-deeper penetration. St. Augustine in his *Confessions* has spoken profoundly on this matter.[62]

But what we have been saying does not transcend the natural, what we call the psychic life. The person who entrusts himself to the mystery of grace and the new birth is given something more. The preaching of St. Paul is interwoven with the message that a new and holy life awakens in the believer. Christ, the risen and transfigured Lord, awakens it in him.

[62]Cf. *Confessions*, Bk. 10, ch. 8 ff.

Here there is an interiority, a depth which lies beyond the merely natural, as far beyond the natural depth of soul as the "realm" where God is enthroned, and where our "glory to God in the highest" seeks Him, and is beyond all thoughts and feelings of natural sublimity. This interiority has been given to us by Baptism, and now Christian practice must lift it beyond the natural world of feeling and thinking.

Let us strive to become silent so that we may learn to be human. The symbol that warns us is already in our world: machines that "speak" to us with human voices. They are interesting, as a result of science and an accomplishment of technology, but they betray — in connection with computers and other machines — a secret desire to deprive man of his dignity. But as soon as man learns really to speak and really to be silent, he becomes inimitable, because then the image of God is revealed in him.

What the machines accomplish is not really speech any more than the accomplishments of the other apparatuses are really thought. In machines, the mechanical forms of speaking and thinking are isolated and placed at the disposal of the operator. They are raised to a degree of speed of which true thinking is not capable and thereby new technological possibilities are created. These are amazing accomplishments of science and technology, but what a temptation to attempt to fathom the real life of man by comparison with the machine and thereby to forget his essential nature. It may help us to understand if we consider that the machine can "talk" but not be silent. It can only stand lifeless. This specter of silence makes us feel at once that its "speaking" also is only a specter. To be silent, to live in silence, is possible only for man.

Let us try again, by means of human life, which is the image of God, to attain to a view of the original. Is it true that the acts of speaking and of keeping silence mean something in connection with God? Is there something in Him for which they can be a symbol? It is indeed so, and this is expressed in two statements of divine Revelation. The first lies in the pronouncement which rings through the whole sacred message, that God alone is God and there is no divinity beside Him. He alone is the Lord, the wholly free and independent one, the eternal, the ever-living, who has and is all.

Before this Supreme One, who transcends all possibilities of thinking and feeling, all images which imply noise or agitation must fail. It is true that the psalmists speak of theophanies that are accompanied by storm and lightning and thunder, and these enable man to surmise the meaning of *omnipotence*, which transcends all created power. But once and for all, God Himself revealed the decisive truth when He called the mighty Elijah, the stormiest of prophets, to the holy Mount Horeb after the tremendous exertions of his struggle against Ahab and Jezebel, and there revealed to the zealous prophet who He was. He commanded him, " 'Go forth and stand upon the mount before the Lord.' And behold the Lord passed, and a great and strong wind before the Lord, overthrowing the mountains, and breaking the rocks in pieces: but the Lord was not in the wind; and after the wind, an earthquake: but the Lord was not in the earthquake; and after the earthquake, a fire: but the Lord was not in the fire; and after the fire, a whisper of a gentle air," and God was therein.[63]

[63]3 Kings 19:11-12 (RSV = 1 Kings 19:11-12).

He was not in the images of crushing forces, but, in a gentle breeze, He revealed Himself to His prophet. So we may carry on the thought: the image of the life of God would be the infinite stillness of an all-embracing silence.

But the New Testament speaks of another image, at the beginning of St. John's Gospel. There we read, "In the beginning was the Word; and the Word was with God and the Word [Itself] was God."[64] At the end of the prologue, the thought is resumed and given a mysterious depth: "No man hath seen God at any time; the only-begotten Son who is in the bosom of the Father, He hath declared Him."[65]

Again we see a glimmer of God's mystery. We are told that in the unicity of God, which permits of no comparison, there is a community; His complete simplicity has a vis-à-vis; His majesty includes a giving and taking. The image for this is the uttering of a word out of silence. This image is then linked with that of the birth of the Son from the Father. The Word is the Son, and "speech" is "birth"; both are incomprehensible.

The first image, that of silence and soundless simplicity, and the second, of speaking birth and community in love, include the mystery of God's life and sacred lordship.

But what a mystery is man also, since in him is reflected, by God's will, the primal glory! And what a task it is to preserve this in its inviolate purity!

[64]John 1:1.
[65]John 1:18.

Justice Before God

One of the first reflections in this book was entitled "Justice." By this word we designated that virtue which seeks to meet other persons, the events of life, and the things of the world in the manner which their nature demands.

But in both the Old and New Testaments, another concept is emphasized: justice before God. When is man just before God? When is he such that his debts are remitted before the Divine Judge — when God receives him into eternal communion with Himself?

The two concepts intertwine. Ethical justice is based upon the truth of natural being, and this has been created by God. This kind of justice is good and is approved by God, the same God who, in the New Testament, tells the believer that it is insufficient. So the two kinds of justice differ, sometimes so much that our immediate sense of justice objects, for example in the parable of the laborers in the vineyard.[66]

Here, at the end of our reflections, we shall try to make clear what Revelation understands by "justice before God,"

[66]Matt. 20:1-16.

being justified in His sight; and in this way, we shall seek to bring everything that we have previously said to a definite conclusion.

We are inclined to consider the ethics of the Old Testament natural and to say that the supernatural — the reception of human activity into the activity of God — is made clear only in the New Testament. But this is not true. What is called "justice" in the Old Testament would not, for example, be understood by Plato, since it rests basically not upon an immediate insight into the nature of things, nor upon the seriousness of a conscience which is determined to follow the good, but upon an act of God, the covenant of Mount Sinai. Hence it belongs to no system of ethics which could be separated from and understood apart from this event. All "merely ethical" judgments of the Old Testament are erroneous.

It is rather like this: God there carries on with men a history which shall build His kingdom on earth. A solemn act, the covenant on Mount Sinai, establishes the existence of the nation which shall carry on the kingdom. Justice here means the fulfillment of that which the covenant demands. First of all, and basically, it means God's own conduct in granting the covenant and binding Himself by it and keeping it. Then it means the conduct of man, which is made possible by God's action — the conduct of man, who knows that he is bound to fulfill the demands of his divine partner in the covenant.

But the binding quality which this covenant possesses in common with all true ethical conduct lies in the universal sovereignty of God, who has begun the building of His kingdom with this nation and in this land, but wishes — as the prophets never wearied of declaring — to spread it over all nations, over the whole earth, even over the whole creation.

So the justice of the Old Testament means a manner of life demanded and made possible by God's grace in the covenant. It consists in God's guidance of history, building the kingdom, and in man's readiness to fit himself into it. Its demands are related to the manifold tasks of life and further developed by the "law," and here they encounter the immediately ethical justice which results from the nature of things and give to this a new meaning.

To fulfill this demand of God required heroic faith and obedience on the part of the people. They renounced entirely all natural politico-social and economic judgment and trusted that God, by His covenant, had promised that the nation as well as the individual would survive and flourish even in this world; that is, they relied upon a continued "miracle."

Hence the man of the Old Testament was always tempted to distrust the miracle of the covenant and to live "like all nations."[67] The tragedy of the Old Testament consisted in the fact that he succumbed to this temptation again and again. The first book of Kings tells of the first instance: "And it came to pass, when Samuel was old, that he appointed his sons to be judges over Israel. . . . And his sons walked not in his ways; but they turned aside after lucre, and took bribes, and perverted judgment. Then all the ancients of Israel being assembled came to Samuel to Ramatha, and they said to him: 'Behold, thou art old, and thy sons walk not in thy ways; make us a king to judge us, as all nations have.' " Samuel was

[67]Ezek. 25:8.

shocked by this defection. "And the Lord said to Samuel: 'They have not rejected thee, but me, that I should not reign over them.' "[68]

In the course of history, the concept of the justice of the old covenant loses its true meaning and turns into that ambiguous pharisaical attitude which Jesus opposes.

In the Sermon on the Mount, He constructs His message on the contrast, "It was said to you . . . but I say to you . . ."[69] Wherein does the new covenant here set forth consist? Evidently, it consists first of all in this: that Jesus places all the emphasis on the interior instead of the exterior and on purity of intention rather than on correctness of action. The whole Sermon on the Mount shows this. But could we also say that now God's covenant separates itself from the single historical instance — that is, the person, the action, and the destiny of Jesus — and spreads out over the whole of humanity? Could it be that the ethical situation hereafter develops between a general moral law revealed by God and a purified but autonomous conscience, and that justice means the purity and perfection with which God's demand is fulfilled?

It is self-evident that an attitude toward life of such sublimity and at the same time so realistic as that proclaimed by Jesus must also contain a structure of general norms and values that can be theoretically grasped. But everything is bound up with reality; every system of ethics, if it does not limit itself to the merely formal, is bound up with reality — the reality of existence as such. In the other case, it is a question of something

---

[68]1 Kings 8:1, 2-7 (RSV = 1 Sam. 8:1, 2-7).
[69]Matt. 5:21-22, 27-28, 31-34, 38-39.

which comes to us only through Revelation and depends upon it, namely, God and His kingdom.

But the term *God* is not to be understood as "the absolute being" or "the basic cause of the world" or in any other philosophical terms, but as "the living one," who is hidden, and who becomes known only through Revelation, or, to put it more exactly, as the God who acts and carries out history — not in the general sense that He, as Creator and Preserver of all existence also guides the actions of men, but a very special history, which also is based upon a covenant: the Incarnation of the Son of God, who has atoned for the sins of mankind and, "in His blood," has made of men the new people of God.[70] From this covenant there arises a new, divinely guided history whose purpose is to realize the new kingdom of God.

This kingdom does not signify any abstract order of values or a generally comprehensible form of human society, but the world of grace and love of the living God and the transformation which everything human — indeed everything created — undergoes therein. The very first message of Jesus announces the approach of this kingdom. In the "fullness of time,"[71] in which the history ripens toward its crisis, it is to be realized, and renewed admonitions and parables bring it close to man. Right action is faith in the growth of this kingdom and love, which serves it in daily activities.

Jesus' message about Providence also does not mean something like the hellenistic world order, but rather the divine guidance of history, which is directed toward the realization of

[70]Matt. 26:28; Luke 22:20.
[71]Mark 1:15.

the holy kingdom, but at the same time the guidance of the destiny of every individual so that the one takes place in and through the other. "Seek ye therefore first the kingdom of God and His justice, and all these things [necessary for life] shall be added unto you."[72]

The justice of God, then, means that He fulfills His promises to man, and the justice of man consists in placing himself within the covenant, seeking God's kingdom first, putting it before all else, and trusting God's holy guidance. The Lord's Prayer expresses the attitude which should prevail here.

Of course, the admonition to justice is combined with the admonition to follow Christ, which includes "taking up the cross."[73] But this, too, is not to be a general ethical attitude of stoic or ascetic nature, but rather the personal relation of the believer to Christ, his Savior. Here again the commandment is stripped of every abstract form and is revealed as the claim of God's love addressed to each individual person.

If we look farther, at the act of God which shall conclude history and give to all existence its eternally valid definition — the Last Judgment — then we see that love of God is set up as the criterion for each man's judgment. But again, this love is not the generally ethical value which results from the character of a human personality as such, but it is love of Christ which expresses and realizes itself in every act of love of neighbor. "For I was hungry and you gave me to eat; I was thirsty and you gave me to drink; I was a stranger and you took me in; [I was] naked and you covered me, sick, and you visited

[72]Matt. 6:33.
[73]Matt. 16:24.

me; I was in prison and you came to me. . . . As long as you did it to one of these my least brethren, you did it to me."[74] It is Christ, then, who steps into every encounter of the believer with his neighbor and operates the mystery of relationship.

And finally that event in which everything — creation, redemption, and sanctification — shall be fulfilled, namely, the birth of "the new man," and the coming into existence of "the new world," is expressed by the revelation of Christ and the eternal consummation of His kingdom: "And I saw a new Heaven and a new earth. For the first Heaven and the first earth were gone, and the sea is now no more. And I saw the holy city, the new Jerusalem, coming down out of Heaven from God, prepared as a bride adorned for her husband. And I heard a great voice from the throne saying, 'Behold the tabernacle of God with men, and He will dwell with them. And they shall be His people, and God Himself with them shall be their God.' "[75]

The final conclusions of this line of thought were drawn by St. Paul. In his lifetime, the true meaning of the old covenant had largely faded from sight. It was generally considered a kind of juristic action in which two parties undertake mutual responsibilities and acquire rights.

Of course, the difference, which results from the sovereignty of God and the humanity of man and which nothing can bridge, was retained. But the nature of the human "achievement," that is, the fulfilling of the law, is emphasized to such an extent that it must lead to the view that by this fulfilling as

[74]Matt. 25:35-40.
[75]Rev. 21:1-3.

such, man is justified before God and acquires a legal claim to the fulfillment of God's promises. The pharisaical doctrine and practice come into being, which include a great serious-ness and constant willingness to take pains and make sacri-fices, but the decisive thing, the fact that everything which comes from God is grace, moves into the background.

Saul of Tarsus, the pupil of the Pharisees, was a man filled with a deep sense of his own sin and a consuming desire for justice, but also a mighty urge toward sanctification through his own power. His letters, especially the letter to the Romans, show how in such a character this urge becomes poisoned and leads to despair. The immediate expression of this *impasse* was the persecution of the early Christian community of which the book of Acts tells us.[76]

The experience on the journey to Damascus,[77] of which the book of Acts also tells brought the solution, and in such a way that Paul realized that there can be no justice through our own actions, but that justice and salvation are both of grace. The whole order of the Old Testament, Paul continues, had the task of showing the nature and enormity of sin and the impos-sibility of justification by human power. Man — both the individual and the race as a whole — is incapable of any action that could please God. Of himself he is capable only of evil.[78]

[76] Acts. 8:3, 9:1-2.

[77] Acts 9:3-8.

[78] Rom. 3 ff. Of course, this train of thought must be accepted as what it is: a definite aspect of the whole situation, carried to the extreme. That the Old Testament also had a very positive character, and that a fruitful effort of man in the task of his own sanctification is

Only one is just: Christ, the Redeemer. Although personally sinless, He took upon Himself the responsibility for human sin and atoned for it. This atonement and the justice that
issues from it He gives to His human brethren by an act of
sovereign grace. It becomes their own through faith and Baptism — the sacrament in which the old sinful life is put to
death and a new life is born: the man who no longer stands in
his own justice but in that of Christ. Thereby, of course, he is
in duty bound and also able to do all of which personal good
will and desire for the fulfillment of God's will are capable.
The mystery of the saving and justifying action of Christ finds
its ultimate expression in the sentence of the letter to the
Galatians, "I live, now not I [as the natural self], but Christ
lives in me."[79]

What Paul proclaims is absolute mystery. Justice in the
Christian sense is the justice of Christ, which is given to the
believer in his rebirth to a new life. How this is possible —
how, to ask a plain question, the moral character or justice of
one person can become the property of another person — can
be answered reasonably only if we understand the whole relation as the fruit of a sovereign divine action, an action in which
the creative power which was first revealed in the conception
and realization of the world, reaches its highest peak.

It is true that the New Testament idea of justice has largely
lost its true meaning in Christian thought. Many circumstances have contributed to this. One was the necessity of

possible, is shown by the letter of St. James and by the whole group
of the "silent ones in the land," to which belonged persons such as
the mother of Jesus, Elizabeth, Zachariah, and others.
[79]Gal. 2:20.

having general norms for moral life, norms which would be comprehensible even to a non-Christian environment. These norms were found by explaining the biblical teaching by means of concepts which belonged to general ethical thought. But the result of this was that the true meaning of what was called "justice" in the Pauline sense faded more and more. Then theology also required concepts with which to build a connected system of ethics. These were found in philosophy, and this also brought it about that what St. Paul meant by *justice* was assimilated to the general notion. And finally the whole Christian Revelation and the life of faith which was based upon it was included in the history of culture, and Christianity was thought of as one epoch of this history, as the working out of an individualistic or an altruistic or a social or some other way of thinking.

In the course of these occurrences, which reciprocally affected each other, there came about what we call the "secularization" of Christianity, an event whose disturbing effects are very evident in our day. In consequence of this, it becomes more and more necessary to distinguish the themes of Revelation from the philosophical and cultural conceptions which were used to explain them, and at the same time to show that the true thought of Revelation is capable of producing effects for human existence which are quite beyond the power of the vague and faded concepts of general ethical thought.

If we seriously consider the personal implications of these thoughts which Revelation brings to us, must not our deepest self-consciousness rebel?

This tells us — and what it says is true, for the glory of our humanity depends upon it — that we are persons. It holds true for each one of us: my deepest consciousness bears witness to the fact that I am a person. Then is it possible that I can be redeemed by the act of another, that is, freed from my guilt, and justified, that is, declared "just" before the absolute judgment? Can God's eternal Son give me a share in His justice, that is, His own personal ethical character?

Guilt is not merely something which hangs upon me; it is not some characteristic that could also be different, but it is bound up with my self in that closeness which we call "responsibility." I cannot free myself from this, however much it burdens me, but I must accept it. And if my finite ethical force is no match for the greatness of this debt, then I must simply remain indebted. For in this debt — and it is this fact that makes it so profound — there lies not only my misfortune, but also my dignity, misused, it is true; for it is only what is done in freedom, and that means in the dignity of the person, that can be called a debt. Hence the question arises: Is it possible that this debt should be removed from me, as the message of salvation states, by another, that is, Jesus Christ?

Likewise "to be just" is a freely willed ethical value belonging to the person. This value is not merely something that is externally, juridically attached to me, but it is also fixed by that strictness which comes from responsibility. From this also I cannot detach myself. For example, I cannot say that an ethical value, no matter how much it appeals to me, shall be attributed to me if I have not realized it in the responsibility of freedom. If I have not done this, I must simply admit, in the honesty of an ethical judgment, that I do not possess this value.

All this gives rise to the following question: Is it possible that the debt can be taken from me in the manner of which the message of salvation speaks, "through another"? And also that the value which stands validly before the absolute judgment can be given to me through this other? Is there any communion which so bridges the distinction between "I" and "not I" that this substitution can take place?

Here lurks a danger to which many — even many good souls — have succumbed, namely, the danger of equating "person" and "absolute person." But the basic character of my human self-experience consists precisely in this fact that I experience myself as person but also as finite, as created, and that means entirely depending upon "the power of another." This seems to involve us in a contradiction.

Two definite considerations lead us out of this difficulty. The first indicates that God is not "I," but simply and in absolute majesty "He," yet at the same time is, in relation to me, not "another" or "the great other," but God the Creator, who is above every category that determines finite creation as such. The second is that we must not think of God's creative act as uniform, no matter to what it is directed, but that He, as act, contains the whole plenitude which belongs to His work as such. God creates mere things by commanding, "It shall be!"; for example, "Be light made, and light was made."[80] But God creates man in "breathing His breath" into the form made of the stuff of earth,[81] which means, in turning personally to him and saying, "Thou, be!"

This is the basis of created personality, and everything depends on man's understanding himself from this viewpoint.

[80]Gen. 1:3.
[81]Gen. 2:7.

The personality of man is not absolute like that of God, but it is finite. His freedom is not autocratic, but it is a gift. His existence is not based upon himself; it is created. The sin that man commits he commits by a freedom bestowed upon him, and he realizes the value of moral integrity through a freedom given to him, not an absolute and original freedom. Similarly, the identity between his own decision and his person is not absolute but finite, and that means that it is a gift.

So when the love of God for lost mankind is so profound that the Creator intervenes in love for His creature, and the eternal Son, sent by the Father, becomes man and takes the responsibility of His brethren upon Himself, He does not deprive them of the dignity of their freedom. He does not place the atonement upon their shoulders like a garment or write above them the verdict of justice like a judicial pronouncement, but a unique identification takes place. The Redeemer bestows His atonement and His justice upon man, yet it remains His own, not man's, accomplishment. Herein is consummated that love which has given man his existence as his very own but as finite and bestowed, just as it gave him his personal freedom and responsibility as really his own but as a gift.

When I say "I," I do not say it autonomously, but as based upon that "thou" which God speaks to me. I say it as truly my own "I," but as coming from God, and so dependent upon the keyword of my existence, which is "I through Him," or more correctly and piously, "I through Thee." In this way, I am also absolved, but through Christ's atonement; I am justified, but through His justice. (These ideas are not deductions from a natural philosophical dialectic of the person, but rather an

Learning the Virtues

attempt to follow through premises and conclusions provided by Revelation.)

What we have said leads to a further question: If the justice which is given to me as a Christian, and which alone is valid before the eternal Judge, is the justice of Christ, then must not everything that we call conscience, responsibility, and moral endeavor be wiped out? Must not this bring about an attitude which is as much indolence as discouragement?

The answer comes from the same line of thought which we have developed: Existence is given to man so that he may take it with a sense of responsibility and use it rightly. It is not really given to him, but it is entrusted to him, just as the world was given to him in the form of a sacred trust, that he might "cultivate it and keep it."[82] So also the justice of Christ is not man's possession, but a trust — the last and most precious gift of God's love placed in the hand of man's freedom that he may "administer" it.[83]

Moreover, the doctrine of Revelation, that man is absolved and justified in Christ, means something active. The justice given by Christ is not merely a juridical adjudication, but a task and a power, and it is realized in the believer who rightly understands it as an urge to do God's will in every way and to work for His kingdom.

So we can understand that the apostle who, more than all others, has proclaimed this mystery, St. Paul, could say of himself, "By the grace of God I am what I am; and His grace in me has not been void, but I have labored more abundantly

[82]Gen. 2:15.
[83]Cf. Matt. 25:14-29.

than they all; yet not I, but the grace of God with me."[84] The whole mystery of grace and its relation to freedom is here expressed, and everything that might be added would only repeat the same thing: as soon as the believer rightly understands the revelation that he exists in the justice of Christ, there awakens in him a great seriousness and he brings forth all the fruits of moral virtue.

Of course, there is also brought about what Christian ethics calls "humility." It is contained in the apostle's words which we have quoted: "not I, but the grace of God with me." And yet he had just said, "I have labored more than they all." This is a continuation of the basic truth of Christian existence which he expresses in the letter to the Galatians when he says, "I live, now not I, but Christ in me."

Hence all Christian action has this twofold character: the seriousness, the readiness, and the efforts that Christ's justice shall bear fruit; but at the same time that which is expressed in the words of Jesus: "When you shall have done all these things, say, 'We are unprofitable servants.' "[85] These two points are together the basis of Christian action. They are also the basis of the last incomprehensible character which belongs to all Christian action, that it is the doer's own and yet a gift — belonging to him, yet the property of Christ.

This thought should be added to all that has been said in the preceding meditations. In order not to endanger the simplicity of our images of the various values, we refrained from working this theme into our account of the virtues. It is left to

[84]1 Cor. 15:10.
[85]Luke 17:10.

the reader to do this in his own meditations. The virtues of which we have spoken, then, become ways in which the justice of Christ becomes fruitful. They receive a new fullness and a new character, that which is meant by the much misused word *holy*.

Perhaps the reader may ask how he is to understand all this. Only human matters can be actually understood. And unless we are rationalists, we know that we are not even wholly successful in understanding those. For man is not simply man, but he is man created and called, the one into whose hand God's confidence has given the world. Therefore he is the finite being, "man," but he is also created, called, and taken into confidence by God — and who could say that he understands that? And when we add the climax, that God Himself steps into the existence of the believer, that He becomes man and, without endangering the personality of the believer, is actually, according to St. Paul, the one living in him — how can this be understood? But we have been given not only natural reason, but believing reason enlightened by Revelation. This enlightened reason understands, insofar as grace and "purity of heart"[86] enable it to do so.

[86]Matt. 5:8.

Romano Guardini
(1885-1968)

Although he was born in Verona, Italy, Romano Guardini grew up in Mainz, Germany, where his father was serving as Italian consul. Since his education and formation were German, he decided to remain in Germany as an adult.

After studying chemistry and economics as a youth, he turned to theology and was ordained to the priesthood in 1910. From 1923 to 1939 (when he was expelled by the Nazis), Father Guardini occupied a chair especially created for him at the University of Berlin as "professor for philosophy of religion and Catholic *Weltanschauung*." After the war, similar positions were created for him — first at the University of Tübingen and then at the University of Munich (1948-63).

Father Guardini's extremely popular courses in these universities won him a reputation as one of the most remarkable and successful Catholic educators in Germany. As a teacher, a writer, and a speaker, he was notable for being able to detect and nurture those elements of spirituality that nourish all that is best in the life of Catholics. After the war, Father

Guardini's influence grew to be enormous, not only through his university positions, but also through the inspiration and guidance he gave to the postwar German Catholic Youth Movement, which enlivened the faith of countless young people.

Father Guardini's writings include works on meditation, education, literature, art, philosophy, and theology. Among his dozens of books, perhaps the most famous is *The Lord*, which has been continuously in print in many languages since its first publication in 1937. Even today, countless readers continue to be transformed by these books, which combine a profound thirst for God with great depth of thought and a delightful perfection of expression. Father Guardini's works are indispensable reading for anyone who wants to remain true to the Faith and to grow holy in our age of skepticism and corrosive doubt.

Sophia Institute

Sophia Institute is a nonprofit institution that seeks to nurture the spiritual, moral, and cultural life of souls and to spread the Gospel of Christ in conformity with the authentic teachings of the Roman Catholic Church.

Sophia Institute Press fulfills this mission by offering translations, reprints, and new publications that afford readers a rich source of the enduring wisdom of mankind.

Sophia Institute also operates two popular online Catholic resources: CrisisMagazine.com and CatholicExchange.com.

Crisis Magazine provides insightful cultural analysis that arms readers with the arguments necessary for navigating the ideological and theological minefields of the day. *Catholic Exchange* provides world news from a Catholic perspective as well as daily devotionals and articles that will help you to grow in holiness and live a life consistent with the teachings of the Church.

In 2013, Sophia Institute launched Sophia Institute for Teachers to renew and rebuild Catholic culture through service to Catholic education. With the goal of nurturing the spiritual, moral, and cultural life of souls, and an abiding respect for the role and work of teachers, we strive to provide materials and programs that are at once enlightening to the mind and ennobling to the heart; faithful and complete, as well as useful and practical.

Sophia Institute gratefully recognizes the Solidarity Association for preserving and encouraging the growth of our apostolate over the course of many years. Without their generous and timely support, this book would not be in your hands.

www.SophiaInstitute.com
www.CatholicExchange.com
www.CrisisMagazine.com
www.SophiaInstituteforTeachers.org

Sophia Institute Press® is a registered trademark of Sophia Institute.
Sophia Institute is a tax-exempt institution as defined by the
Internal Revenue Code, Section 501(c)(3). Tax I.D. 22-2548708.

Printed in March 2026
by Rotomail Italia S.p.A., Vignate (MI) - Italy